Roy Kendall

The Onion
at the End

Salamander Street

PLAYS

First published in 2020 by Salamander Street Ltd.
(info@salamanderstreet.com)

Printed and bound in Great Britain

10 9 8 7 6 5 4 3 2 1

The Onion At The End was first produced in February 2018 by the Sarah Thorne Theatre in association with the Terence Rattigan Society with the following cast:

BOB FIRST	Alexander Hulme
JIMMY LAST	Stephen Martin-Bradley
DILLY WILLIAMS	Johanna Pearson-Farr
TEDDY HOSKINS	Edward Broomfield
ROSE HOSKINS	Lainey Shaw
DAN SANDFORD	Clive Greenwood

CREATIVES

Director	Michael Friend
Producer	Michael Wheatley-Ward
Designer	Caitlin Line
Sound Effects	David Gilbrook
Stage Manager	Andrea Vigo
Deputy Stage Manager	Terrie Wheatley-Ward
Lighting/Sound Control	Sarah Bicknell

The action of the play takes place over the course of a pantomime season in Birkenhead and a summer season in Southport, Lancashire, in the early 1930s

The Onion at the End won the Terence Rattigan Society Award for a New Play for the Theatre

ACT ONE

SCENE ONE

A small dressing room in the Argyll Theatre, Birkenhead, in the early 1930s.

Distant sound of audience applause. A pit band strikes up a play-out. It lasts for one chorus and then concludes with a flourish accompanied by some further but sporadic applause. Silence.

Then the door bursts open and **BOB SUMMERBEE** *appears, slightly out of breath. He is a balding, slightly overweight, middling to large Yorkshire man in his mid thirties. He is dressed as an Arab sheikh.*

BOB: Well that was an uphill battle. In the mud. Without a weapon.

> *[He flops down in front of his mirror and takes off his turban.*
>
> *At this moment* **JIMMY LAST** *strides in, shutting the door behind him. He is a Londoner in his early thirties. He gives the general impression of being an educated barrow boy.* **JIMMY** *wears a rat costume with an ermine cloak, a crown and a chain of office.]*

JIMMY: Will someone please release me from this show!

BOB: Stamina! That's what you need, flower.

JIMMY: What happened to our Sinbad? Did you see? His nose was all bloody at the curtain call.

BOB: He tripped over the back legs of the camel.

JIMMY: The camel tripped him, you mean?

BOB: That's because panto camels have short dicks and long memories.

JIMMY: Will you undo me please?

BOB: I'm not your dresser, Jimmy.

JIMMY: I did ask nicely. It's so much easier if you do it.

> *He turns around and* **BOB** *reluctantly obliges.*

BOB: This tail could do with a wash.

JIMMY: It's only got to go till Saturday.

BOB: I still don't understand why King Rat gets to be Lord Mayor of London. Doesn't make any sense to me. A banker perhaps.

JIMMY: That's show business. When I was in *Robinson Crusoe* last year the director had me wearing gloves. Can you tell me what Man Friday was doing wearing white gloves? And crooning in an American accent through a microphone?

BOB: *(Of the costume.)* You can do that bit.

He resumes his seat. **JIMMY** *sits next to him with his back to the mirror and slips off his costume as:*

Next panto season – if there is one the way business is going – I'm trying out for dame.

JIMMY: You should. You've got the build.

BOB: Just tell me where you'll be playing, and I'll be on other bloody side of bloody country.

JIMMY: Okay then, Bob, what would you do if they offered you dame here and I was playing just over the water in Liverpool? At the Hippodrome say.

BOB: I'd shoot myself. *(He looks up to the ceiling.)* Please, God, never again. Never Birkenhead. Amen.

JIMMY swivels round and begins taking off his make up. He cleans himself up, bit by bit, as the scene progresses.

You're surely not taking off all that slap?

JIMMY: Don't have a choice, do I?

BOB: You don't usually.

JIMMY: I'm popping out to see a man about a dog.

BOB: Oh, you mean a greyhound.

He takes out a vacuum flask and an old Oxo tin from underneath his dressing table.

Well, I reckon it's teatime. Let's see what Mrs Moneypincher's made me today. I'll tell you something though, Jimmy, the show may be looking more jaded than the bull that got locked in the milking parlour, but one good thing happened out there this afternoon…

JIMMY: Go on, give me hope.

BOB: Did you see my routine with Miss Turkish Delight?

JIMMY: No. I was having a fag.

BOB: She made it! We've only been playing since – when? -- late November and here we are, the end of March, and she got the patter word for word for the first time.

> *(**JIMMY** grins, but whether he is amused we have no way of telling. **BOB** delves into his tin and pulls a face.)*

Oh my sainted trouser bottoms.

JIMMY: What?

BOB: She's given me rabbit sandwiches again.

JIMMY: Let me try a bite.

BOB: You can sod off. You breed your own bunnies. What's your landlady made you?

JIMMY: I'm having something out before the show this evening. Giving my taste buds a little holiday away from the grind of daily fish paste.

BOB: Paying for it with your winnings, eh, flower?

JIMMY: Mind your business. And please don't put that on my side. If you wish to keep your side looking like a bric-a-brac stall after an earth tremor, that's up to you. But I need my side to be…

BOB: In order?

JIMMY: Neater than that side certainly.

BOB: And what's your ukulele doing on my side?

JIMMY: Good question. Put it back when you've finished with it.

> *He leans over and reclaims his instrument.*

> *__BOB__ ignores this as he chews away on his sandwich – much to **JIMMY**'s disgust at his unorthodox eating habits. **JIMMY** meanwhile continues taking off his make up, whiskers, etc.*

BOB: You got any tricks up your sleeve for the last night?

JIMMY: Nah, not yet. Had other things on me mind. How about you?

BOB: Got three. One for the stage manager. I'm going to disappear a few of his props before he goes to set them for Sinbad. One for the band. I shall be singing a completely different song to the arrangement they're playing.

JIMMY: Don't you always?

BOB: And a third one for you.

JIMMY: How will you manage that? We never meet on stage.

BOB: We will.

JIMMY: You've just warned me now.

BOB: *(Mock sinister.)* But you've got to recognize me.

> **JIMMY** *gives him a wary grin.*

So…you got anything lined up for the summer yet?

JIMMY: Couple of possibilities, yeah.

BOB: Nothing definite though?

JIMMY: You?

BOB: Same. It's the bloody Depression.

JIMMY: Too right! When's the government going to do its job, like we have to do ours?

BOB: All right, all right, everyone's suffering. Frankly, I'm surprised there's anyone who can afford to go to seaside these days.

JIMMY: So what'll you do if you can't get a booking?

BOB: Go painting the town I suppose.

JIMMY: And how d'you afford that?

BOB: What, a paint brush?

JIMMY: Eh?

BOB: I used to be a house painter so I can again if I can find a ladder with rungs that move me up and down.

JIMMY: Paint's expensive, matey. Can people afford it these days?

BOB: Okay, okay, so what'll you do?

JIMMY: God only knows. I've got no training. Believe it or not, I did actually go to grammar school. Passed my matric. But without funds university might just as well have been a pot of gold at the end of a rainbow. So I took a job in a library but got the sack for being too familiar with a colleague in the Sports & Hobbies section. Then I got work in a garage – in the stores – Ford dealership. Became a walking encyclopaedia of Ford part numbers. But then, praise be, I started winning a few talent contests. So, unlike you with your pot of paint, I perform without a safety net.

BOB: You know, I would have put money on you having been a gentlemen's outfitter.

JIMMY: And I'd have bet you were a miner.

BOB: Not bloody likely! No, no, I've seen too much. My whole ruddy family lives down a mine-shaft. Well, my father was invalided out with emphysema but my brother, poor sod, is still chipping away down there. And I've an unmarried sister who works at mine in the offices. Another who's married to a miner. And Jane, my third sister, got out and married a coalman.

JIMMY: So you're the black sheep of the family?

BOB: That I am, but they're so covered in coal dust they can't see the difference.

There is a knock on the dressing room door.

JIMMY: Show your face, whoever you are.

> **DYLYS 'DILLY' WILLIAMS** *enters. She is 19, appealing, busty, sharp and full of beans. She is dressed as a showgirl ready for a night in a harem and carries a large greetings card and a tin.*

Your face I said.

She sticks her tongue out at him.

BOB: Ah, but here she is ladies and gentlemen! From the West of Wales, full of Eastern Promise, Dilys – 'Seven Veils on Sunday, Two on Saturday Night' – Williams!

DILLY: And you can get knotted.

BOB: Oh, come on, Dilly, I'm your greatest fan. You got every syllable of the patter right this afternoon, my little darling.

DILLY: Because at last you fed me the lines properly. But even then that little shit of a stage manager – if you'll pardon the pun – had the cheek to tell me afterwards that there's still room for improvement. God, I've been in the business *eighteen months* now and people are still telling me what to do!

JIMMY: Never mind, Dilly, you come up here to give Bob a heart attack?

DILLY: I shall ignore that. Now, sign this. And put your life savings in here.

BOB: Your birthday, is it, Dilly?

DILLY: It's for Ernie. I don't think he'll be able to carry on after this show. Poor love's messing up left, right and centre.

BOB: But what'll he do? He's only ever lived in theatrical digs. Where will he go?

DILLY: That's the problem. So let's give him a bit of a send off.

BOB: What, to the workhouse?

DILLY: Wherever, I don't know.

BOB: The poor man really will be playing Baron Hard-Up.

DILLY: I just thought a little whip round would be a nice idea.

JIMMY: It is, Dilly. Where do I sign?

DILLY: Oh no. *(Of the tin.)* No donation *(Of the greetings card.)* no signature.

JIMMY: You're a hard woman.

DILLY: Got to be. You'd never believe the excuses people have been making for leaving their money back in their digs. Including our so-called star. But… *(She shakes the tin vigorously.)* I prise it out of them.

BOB: You should have come to us first, we'd have got your tin rattling.

DILLY: I would have, if I didn't need a pack horse to get up to your dressing room.

> *She gives the tin two shakes as if to say "boom-boom". The men reluctantly find her some money and sign the card as:*

JIMMY: Hey, Dilly, got anything lined up for the summer?

DILLY: Might have. How about you?

JIMMY: Well, chance of a season at…Herne Bay.

DILLY: Firm offer?

JIMMY: Not yet.

DILLY: What about you, Bob?

BOB: Still negotiating.

DILLY: With?

BOB: For an agent.

DILLY: Right.

JIMMY: So, come on, Dill, what's in your date-book then?

DILLY: Oh…you don't want to know.

BOB: Oh yes we do. No, let me guess. The Bird's Nest, Scunthorpe.
  JIMMY: The Pier Pavilion, Cleethorpes.

DILLY: The Winter Gardens, Southport.

> *(The men go quiet.)*

BOB: *(Taken aback but genuine.)* Good for you.

JIMMY: Yeah. Part of Sandford's empire, isn't it?

DILLY: I…think it is, yes. One of his No.2 theatres. But it's a damn sight better than this No.3, and one day soon might lead to a No.1.

BOB: So which mathematician got you this, Dilly?

DILLY: I got it off my own bat thank you very much.

BOB: And…what, you going t'be head girl of the troupe again?

DILLY: Um, no, I think they're finding a little more for me.

BOB: That's brilliant. They don't need a comic, by any chance?

JIMMY: Or a crooner who does jokes?

DILLY: No…sorry, lads, I don't think so. As far as I know they're only short of a double act.

BOB: Really?

DILLY: Yeah, top of the bill too.

JIMMY: What?! Bit late in the day for getting a tip-top act.

DILLY: I guess.

BOB: But *why* a double? Why *can't* they just have a comic?

JIMMY: Or, better, a singer, comedian, tap dancer, top quality all-round entertainer? Would you not say?

DILLY: Yes, you're brilliant, Jimmy. But Mr. Sandford requires a double – I believe – because he had a double that's just left the organization on the double.

JIMMY: And they'd signed?

DILLY: No. Luckily for them. Or poor Mr. Sandford would've had to have dragged them through the courts. It's Eddie & Freddie we're talking about. No, they got a slot on radio before they signed and pissed off – if you'll pardon the pun. I mean, what an unprofessional thing to do!

BOB: Terrible.

JIMMY: So…there's a spot up for grabs?

DILLY: Well, as far as I know it hasn't been filled.

BOB: Do you think we could audition for it?

DILLY: Are you kidding? The only thing you two have in common is that you share the same dressing room.

BOB: That's not true. We also have in common the fact that we'll both be out of work next week. And if there's only one job going... Worth a try I'd say. Wouldn't you, Dilly?

DILLY: Don't ask me. Only you boys know what you can put up with. I know I couldn't put up with a partner sharing the limelight. If I was famous that is.

JIMMY: Which you will be.

DILLY: You're damn right I will. Now, I must go and get this tin filled up before I freeze my fundamentals.

(She goes to the door. Of the card and tin.)

Thanks for this. At least it shows we mean well.

BOB: Don't you want a quick snifter?

DILLY: Mmm...no, I'll pop back when I'm done, then you can warm me up.

BOB: So...do you reckon you could get us an in? Tell us...who to call?

DILLY: Well...if you can knock an act together, yeah. Suppose. But it would have to be quick.

BOB: We could always say we'd worked together in the past.

DILLY: Say what you like, but you'd have to make Mr. Sandford laugh.

JIMMY: Did you make him laugh?

DILLY: I'm not a comedienne.

(She goes. Pause.)

BOB: Well...there's a turn up.

JIMMY: Mm. To quote Sinbad's immortal line, you never know what's round the next pyramid.

BOB: Dilly in Southport! She's a good-looker but I wouldn't have said she was *that* talented.

JIMMY: Well, she says she got the summer season off her own bat.

BOB: Her own back more like. I think she's up to something with old Sandford.

JIMMY: Why would he go for a pretty, vivacious, young, long-legged thing like her?

BOB: So, it might just be worth the whistle. *(Pause.)* You and me. *(Gritting his teeth.)* Teaming up.

JIMMY: What a grubby thought!

BOB: We wouldn't have to live in each other's pockets. Just work together.

JIMMY: But on what? We'll have to audition. We haven't got any bleeding material.

BOB: We'll knock some off. There're still fifteen theatres in Liverpool, that many if not more in Manchester, how's he going to know where a bit of patter comes from?

JIMMY: And which double do you suggest we steal a routine from?

BOB: You leave that one to the Artful Dodger here. I must give this robe a bit of air before the evening show. Smells like a fishmonger's flannel.

(He changes into his dressing gown as.)

Now, Jimmy, just think about it. Where's your crooning going to get you? In reality. You don't, surely, want to go back to a black face act? And in any case you can't do *The Jazz Singer* cos it's been done. As I see it you're going nowhere, but only because there's nowhere to go. And I sympathize. Look at me. Look around you. I've gone from the pits to the pits. I want a taste of the big-time. Even a lick would be something. I'm sick to death of being a light comedian. Taking the second spot. Warming up audiences. Then handing them over to the top of the bill, especially when it's a heavy comic of the Max Miller variety. Gawd, that galls me. I've got nothing against Max mind you, except that he's the stingiest sod who ever walked the earth. Come on, Jim. We'll tell the Guv'nor we've worked together in the past. And then it's Southport here we come! *And then* it's the Liverpool Hippodrome or a No.1 in Blackpool or it could even be – ta-ra! – the London Palladium!

JIMMY: And then?

BOB: We've a passport to radio. You've got the voice. I've got the looks!

*(**JIMMY** is forced to laugh.)*

Our own radio show perhaps. (Almost a whisper) And then…it could be America. Hollywood. Imagine it! If we get this right we could tread in the footsteps of other English comics like Charlie Chaplin – he's from your way – and Stan Laurel –he's from here abouts – and make films and have swimming pools and live a swanky life. That Bob Hope chap who's just making his mark with Bing whatever-his-name-is. He's from England you know. But first stop Southport, the Paris of the North!

(Pause.)

So are you in?

JIMMY: Let's talk it through. Carefully.

BOB: I thought you were off out to see a man about a dog.

JIMMY: I can manage without.

BOB: There you are. You've made some money already by not gambling it away.

JIMMY: And we'll do without the sermons, thank you.

BOB: Okay then, flower, where d'you think we should begin?

JIMMY: Well…as I see it the best double acts…like Abbott & Costello and Laurel & Hardy…get their laughs from being opposites. What would you say?

BOB: I'd say we've cracked it already then!

JIMMY: …yeah, but I'm talking opposites that still kind of…connect.

BOB: Like?

JIMMY: Like…Rich & Poor.

BOB: Okay, if you want to be the poor character, fine. I'm not being Poor. I've been poor enough for long enough. Aye, you be that one. But it won't do you any favours with the ladies.

JIMMY: What about Drunk & Sober?

BOB: Too close to home.

JIMMY: Or North & South? Then neither of us would have to learn another accent.

BOB: There was an Englishman, an Irishman and a Northerner. No thanks.

JIMMY: Town & Country then. You could be the country bumpkin and I could be the man about town.

BOB: I don't fancy that. Stuck forever with a piece of straw between my teeth. Nah. But, *but*, BUT…how's about Large & Little?

JIMMY: Don't be daft. You're not large enough and I'm not little enough.

BOB: You could diet and I could stuff my face.

JIMMY: Got it! What about Daft & Clever? No, Daft & Smart. That has a real ring to it.

BOB: Which one would you be?

JIMMY: Oh, come on.

BOB: Smart I suppose. Well, you can sod off.

JIMMY: You could get brilliant laughs acting stupid.

BOB: And you could get smart-arsed laughs putting me down.

JIMMY: All right then, let's both be idiots, but you be the bigger idiot.

BOB: No, no, no, no, no, it's comic and feed we're talking here. No negotiation.

JIMMY: Oh, so you'd just like me to be second banana?

BOB: Only where jokes are concerned! But when we sing and dance… you are first banana. Prize banana if you want. Bloody hell!

>   *(Silence.)*

>   You up for it or not?

JIMMY: *(After a beat.)* Not.

>   *(There is a knock on the dressing room door.)*

BOB: Come in.

>   *(DILLY enters with greetings card and tin. She now has a colourful jacket or blazer around her shoulders.)*

DILLY: It's only little me.

BOB: Ah, it's Our Lass from Llandudno!

DILLY: Conway. You know it's Conway.

BOB: Sorry, Dill. Slipped my mind.

DILLY: I think I got everyone. Apart from the snake lady.

BOB: But she's a lovely person. I can't believe she wouldn't contribute.

DILLY: I'm not going in there with those pythons. And for all I know she's got the bloody crocodile in that dressing room as well.

BOB: No she keeps that in a bath under the stage.

JIMMY: It's right below the trap, isn't it, Bob?

DILLY: Oh, don't say that! That's where I sing my big number.

JIMMY: Well, you think of that croc and it might put you in tune, Dilly.

DILLY: Oh sod off.

BOB: Take no notice. He's just a miserable git. Whisky then?

DILLY: Yeah, why not?

> (**BOB** *pours* **DILLY** *a very small whisky. She has to hold up her glass to see the contents. He pours a more generous measure for himself and an in-between amount for* **JIMMY**.)

So, got yourselves an act sorted out?

BOB: No, Mr. High and Mighty here won't play ball.

JIMMY: We've just got different ideas.

DILLY: Well, your funeral, lads. Work's work I say. It's like the arctic out there at the moment. But if you can get a sledge from somewhere else, a Happy Christmas to you.

JIMMY: In any case, who's saying Sandford'll give us the job?

DILLY: Who's saying he won't? There's no one else up for it.

BOB: How d'you know?

DILLY: *(Tapping the side of her nose.)* Trust me. I keep my ear to the ground.

BOB: I hope that's all you keep there, Dilly.

DILLY: That's enough of that smut.

JIMMY: So you're going to be…what exactly?

DILLY: I've got promotion. I'm going to be a soubrette. The soubrette. Been promised my own song in each half. With backing. A dance choreographed just for me. And little parts, if needed, in sketches and routines. Are you reading me, boyos? Come on, get me first before anyone else does.

BOB: Ooh, what a wicked thought.

DILLY: We can sit on the sands and twiddle our toes most mornings…

JIMMY: How many shows a day then?

DILLY: Two. And three if wet. And three changes of bill over the season.

BOB: Well, I say it's better than working down a mine. Or begging.

DILLY: I don't see the problem. All you need are a few songs, a few jokes and a sentimental ending. Oh, and some personality.

BOB: We've…got a routine. Haven't we, Jimmy?

JIMMY: *(After a beat.)* Just the one.

DILLY: Well, do that. Like me to fix up the audition?

BOB: We say go for it. Don't we, Jim? We do apparently.

DILLY: Righty-o. *(Sing song.)* Will do.

> *(She drains the last dribble of whisky out of her glass, puts the glass down and gets up.)*

BOB: Thanks, Dilly.

JIMMY: Yup…thanks.

DILLY: Well, I say, when opportunity knocks, open your bleedin' door – if you'll pardon the pun.

> *(She opens the door with a flourish and exits with card and tin.)*

BOB: Lovely girl.

JIMMY: A cracker.

BOB: Sanford is having her.

JIMMY: And three times a day if wet.

BOB: Right then, let's get this show on the road. And what say we pop out for a jar – just so we can think straight?

JIMMY: Whatever.

BOB: *(Starting to get dressed, etc.)* Jim, working together really is better than being unemployed at such a dreadful bloody time.

JIMMY: Runs it close.

BOB: Only…let's get one thing clear before the off. I really would rather starve than be your stooge. (More conciliatory) It wouldn't work.

JIMMY: *(A beat, then.)* Okay. But I do the singing and the dancing and all the comic choreography.

BOB: And I'm *your* stooge in that area. Fair enough?

> *(He offers his hand. Another beat. **JIMMY** shakes.)*

JIMMY: But we still need an angle…

BOB: …true…

JIMMY: Rightio, what about we take the tack of being Slow and Fast? I mean in everything. Words. Business. Thought processes…

BOB: I'm catching up but I'm still not quite with you.

JIMMY: Exactly! My character would be, like, the minute hand of a clock and yours like the hour hand.

BOB: I'll give you a back-hand in a minute. Slow and Fast my arse! Tell you what. Let's try putting the condom before the erection.

JIMMY: Go on, show me a magic trick.

BOB: Let's think of a name first and then work backwards to the premise.

JIMMY: Last & Summerbee then.

BOB: Summerbee & Last maybe. Nah, still doesn't work. Doesn't give people a sense of what's to come?

JIMMY: Does Abbott & Costello?

BOB: I think it does actually. Costello is a bit of a clownish name. *(With an Italian accent.)* Costello. *(With a Brooklyn accent.)* Costello.

JIMMY: All right then – The Brylcream Brothers.

BOB: Oh leave off. I'd have to tidy myself up.

JIMMY: Right, I've got it! I've *really* got it.

BOB: Go on.

JIMMY: First & Last.

BOB: But you're name's Last, Jimmy, and my name's not First.

JIMMY: It would be First if you *were* First.

BOB: But I'm Summerbee.

JIMMY: And I'd be second billing if you were First.

BOB: But I'm not.

JIMMY: But you could be. You could always be First. Bob First.

BOB: I don't want to be Mr. Frigging First, thank you very much!

JIMMY: Better to be First than Last, surely? Come on, you hate playing second fiddle.

BOB: Fiddle my backside! Why have I got to change my name?

JIMMY: All right then, you be Bob Last. I'll be James First. I'll get first billing.

BOB: No, no, no, no, no. It would be stupid you changing your name.

JIMMY: Ah, so, First, we agree at last. Got the idea?

> *(Pause.)*

BOB: Mmmmm.

> *(There is a vigorous knocking on the dressing room door. **DILLY** rushes in.)*

DILLY: Everyone on stage! Everyone on stage! Emergency!

> *(She immediately turns and exits.)*

JIMMY: *(Calling after her.)* What's up, Dill?

DILLY: *(From the corridor.)* One of the snakes has gone missing!

> *Then men look warily around the room and hurriedly exit.*
>
> *Lights fade.*

SCENE TWO

The parlour of a seaside lodging house in Southport, Lancashire.

The room looks much like any similar guest house of the period, except that signed photographs of previous guests adorn the walls. Doors lead off to kitchen, front room and hall. A flight of stairs leads from the parlour to unseen bedrooms above. Although doors and stairs need to be practical, the general effect need not be too realistic.

A clock begins striking eleven. After a few chimes a young boy, **TEDDY HOSKINS***, pokes his head out of the front room and looks around, then ventures slowly into the parlour. He has a stamp album under his arm and wears pyjamas. He is fourteen years old but looks twelve and occasionally sounds nearer to ten. He makes his way in an agitated but excited manner to the window and in so doing is seen to have a limp.*

Seeming to become disappointed after some moments of waiting, he moves away from the window, sits in the armchair and opens his stamp album.

A beat. Then a car is heard pulling up outside the house. Its doors open and slam and voices are heard off, followed by the sound of a key in a lock and a door opening. **TEDDY** *goes tense with expectancy. Then, when the voices seem about to burst into the room, he closes his album with a snap and quickly disappears whence he came.*

JIMMY *and* **BOB** *enter, each with a suitcase in one hand and a bag in another.* **JIMMY** *has his ukulele tied to the outside of his bag.*

As they are looking around the room **ROSE HOSKINS** *appears in the doorway behind them, taking off her gloves and hat. She is in her late thirties, and though perhaps a little on the plump side is still in good shape. She is a lower middle class woman with a veneer of gentility, which can become a trifle overcooked like the meals she serves.*

ROSE: Suitcases in the hall please.

> *The men turn round and go out obediently with their luggage, returning empty-handed.*

And coats.

They go out again. As they re-appear in the doorway.

And hats.

They disappear from view once more. **ROSE**, *her own coat now removed, steps into the room from the hall, followed in turn by* **BOB** *and* **JIMMY**. *Though travel-worn, we see in an instant that* **JIMMY** *is a more dapper dresser than* **BOB**.

BOB: Sorry about that, Mrs Hoskins.

ROSE: You'll learn. Do have a seat.

BOB *appears to be eyeing a comfortable-looking armchair, but* **ROSE** *points to the sofa. The men move to it and sit one at each end. She looks at them intently.*

First & Last, eh?

JIMMY and **BOB:** *(Together.)* That's us! The Men from the Ministry of Mirth!

ROSE: I've not heard of you.

JIMMY: We're a...an up and coming act.

ROSE: Good. The business needs new blood in times like these. If you're better than average you can go up on this wall.

BOB: And if we're not?

ROSE: I'll still have a photo. And you can go up with the other ones in the lavatory.

BOB: Oh! Fate worse than death, eh, Jimmy?

JIMMY: It certainly is, Bob.

ROSE: *(Proudly.)* But I'll have you know it is an *inside* lavatory. I only offer the best in this house.

BOB: Well, that's put me in the right mood, Mrs Hoskins.

ROSE: Of course, it's included in the price. Now, I suppose you're both hungry?

BOB: I could have eaten the taxi driver.

JIMMY: Train was so late they'd stopped serving. Restaurant car had signs up saying Trespassers Will Be Prosecuted.

ROSE: Yes, well, an hour I waited on that station.

JIMMY: Truth is we got delayed at Crewe.

ROSE: Mr. First, if I had a pound for every time I've heard that I could buy a season ticket to Timbuktu.

JIMMY: No, he's Mr. First.

(BOB gives a mock salute.)

ROSE: (to BOB.) You don't look like a Mr. First I must say. But then again I don't think you look like a Mr. Last either.

JIMMY: Erm, why not just call us…(he indicates.) Bob and Jimmy?

ROSE: That does seem sensible. Though normally I only call my guests by their first names on their second stay. That's if they're good enough to get another booking. I'm Rosemary Hoskins by the way. But Mrs Hoskins will do fine. Welcome to Southport.

(The men mumble a suitable response.)

Now, I've put something in the oven before I left, but it's probably shrivelled up by now. One of my special puddings. Would you like to try some?

BOB and **JIMMY:** *(Together.)* Ooh, would we?

ROSE: Well, would you?

JIMMY: We would.

ROSE: So, make yourselves at home. Feet on the pouffe if you care to – as long as you take your shoes off – and I'll start serving up. (As she goes out into the kitchen.) I'll take you up to your room after supper.

JIMMY: *(Appalled.)* Room? Are we sharing?

ROSE: *(Off.)* You don't have to. I've got a spare. But separates are extra.

BOB: Bleedin' heck.

JIMMY: Extra, extra, we'll go for extra.

ROSE: *(Off.)* Your choice.

> **JIMMY** and **BOB** *look at each other, clearly wondering what on earth they are doing in this guest house and probably in Southport too. The very thought appears to send their minds off in different directions. In the process,* **BOB**'s *attention is caught by the front room door which* **TEDDY**, *on the edge of* **BOB**'s *eyeline, is slowly opening.* **BOB** *half-stands as an automatic reaction. This movement is enough to make* **TEDDY** *quickly close the door.*

BOB: Mrs Hoskins?

ROSE: *(Off.)* Yes?

BOB: Is there anyone else staying here?

ROSE: *(Off.)* No.

BOB: Oh.

> *He turns to look at the door again then sinks back onto the sofa. Awkward moment between* **JIMMY** *and* **BOB** *who are clearly not content in each other's company.* **JIMMY** *gets up and wanders over to where the bulk of framed photographs line the walls.*

JIMMY: I see you've had lots of comics lodging here, Mrs Hoskins.

ROSE: *(Off, proudly.)* I have indeed. Funny ones some of them.

JIMMY: And singers. A few of these are big names now.

ROSE: *(Off.)* That's right. Just think. You'll be sleeping in the same beds they slept in.

JIMMY: Hope they're not the same sheets!

ROSE *(Off.)* I'll ignore that.

JIMMY: "For all our yesterdays and hopes for tomorrows." "Memories always…"

ROSE: *(Off, dubiously.)* Yes, well…

JIMMY: You don't seem to have had many – any – spec. *(Pronounced 'spesh'.)* acts.

ROSE: *(Off.)* Well, I have, but they don't tend to make the second round.

BOB: End up in the lavatory, eh?

ROSE: *(Off.)* They do. In any case, I won't have jugglers in the house. Too light-fingered for my liking. And as for acrobats… The last time I had acrobats here you'll never guess what they got up to.

JIMMY: I think I could at a pinch.

ROSE: *(Off.)* Dirty beasts. I mean, I have a broad mind but it'll only stretch so far. And I also have a young boy in the house. Teddy his name is. You'll meet him tomorrow. Got to think of him.

> (**BOB**'s head turns towards the front room door.)

That's why I won't have any messing about upstairs.

JIMMY: Then why didn't you say that to the acrobats?

ROSE: *(Off.)* I did. And they said they weren't upstairs they were *on* the stairs. Cheeky so-and-so's. Spoil it for everyone else. Okay, if you'd like to sit yourselves at the table…

> *(BOB is there almost before she has finished speaking.* **JIMMY** *follows in a more leisurely fashion as* **ROSE** *comes in with a steaming dish.)*

Here we are. Rice pudding!

BOB: Ah...

JIMMY: Mmm...

ROSE: This'll fill your tummies. There's jam in the pot. Just help yourselves. Yes, the pudding's a little bit congealed...but not too bad. I'll give it a stir. Smells all right. Yes, that's more like it. If you'll pass me your plates... Two spoonfuls? Three?

JIMMY: Three please.

ROSE: My, you are hungry! And you...?

BOB: The same.

ROSE: Hoh! You boys are going to eat me out of house and home. Now, come on, get stuck in. Don't wait on ceremony – to coin a phrase -- and don't burn your mouths. Right, I'll just put kettle on.

> *She picks up the dish and takes it out into the kitchen. The men watch it go disconsolately then begin eating. It is clearly not the best meal they have ever had but their hunger soon ge ts the better of them.*

ROSE: *(Off.)* How is it?

BOB: Oh, it's lovely, Mrs Hoskins, it's lovely.

> **ROSE** *re-appears in the doorway.*

ROSE: Well, you'll get a hot meal every evening after the show – dumplings, suet puddings, that kind of thing – and sandwiches and a flask of tea to take to the theatre every day. And little extras if you're good.

BOB: You don't keep rabbits, do you, Mrs H?

ROSE: Rabbits? Certainly not.

BOB: I can't tell you how pleased I am to hear that. And snakes? Do you keep snakes?

ROSE: Rabbits? Snakes? What is this?

JIMMY: We had a problem with a missing python at our last booking. We all went to look for it, couldn't find it, and when we came back it was wrapped around our dressing table mirror.

ROSE: Don't worry about that here. You haven't got a dressing table.

BOB: Well, that solves that.

JIMMY: Ooh, this is going down a real treat. A big thank you from the bottom of our stomachs.

ROSE: Well, thank you, kind sir. So…as I said in my letter, it's two pounds ten shillings a week for the two of you, all in. Or it would be. It's three guineas now you're each requiring a room to yourself. Is that agreed or would you like to try somewhere else?

The men make signals of agreement and continue eating.

Now, as we're talking business, let's just go through the other rules of the house. Your rooms are your own. But as I said, no hanky panky. And the parlour here is all yours for the use of – which, of course, you'll share with Teddy and me. You can use the kitchen but you won't need to. I don't have a phone but I've taken account of that in the price. If you have an emergency, Mrs Harris over in the blue house has a phone, which she'll probably let you use. I don't mind you rehearsing here, as long as I'm not in. But any breakages will come out of your deposit. What else? Oh yes, don't worry about the taxi fare from the station…

BOB: …that's very kind…

ROSE: …I'll add that to your first week's rent. But you'll like it here. It's comfy. And it's near the theatre. So, all fair in love and war – to coin another phrase?

JIMMY: Sounds like a home from home, Mrs Hoskins.

ROSE: Thank you, Bob.

JIMMY: Jimmy.

ROSE: Jimmy. Oh yes, one more thing. I hope to God you don't find a draft in the house, because I just cannot bear drafts. But if you do, you know your duty.

JIMMY: Er, do we?

ROSE: You make a note of the exact location where you felt the draft in the visitors' book.

JIMMY: And if I felt it around my posterior?

ROSE: I'll do what I always do and plug it with some putty.

*(**JIMMY** looks suitably chastened.)*

BOB: And…(he points to the front room door.) what about that room? Can we use that?

ROSE: No, that is Teddy's room, which is out of bounds, which is also taken account of in the price. No, Teddy has…a problem with the stairs… *(Lowering her voice.)* and a few other things. So he sleeps down here so that I can keep an eye on him. But don't go thinking he's helpless. For one thing he's fourteen years old (lowering her voice even more.), a very young fourteen but perfectly okay for me to leave for an hour while I'm down at the station. I don't know why I'm whispering, he's asleep now anyway.

TEDDY: *(Off.)* No I'm not.

ROSE: Oh, Teddy, Teddy, I told you to go to sleep.

TEDDY: *(Off.)* I did. But I woke up again.

ROSE: Oh well, come and say hello to the gentlemen.

> **TEDDY** *comes into the room. He looks both nervous and excited. The men continue with their meal as best they can during the following exchange.*

Now…these are our guests for the summer. Shake hands. This is… Mr. First…yes? And this is Mr. Last?

TEDDY: Are they your real names?

ROSE: Don't be so rude, Teddy.

JIMMY: It's all right. It's not a secret. I am really James Last, but my friend here is really Robert Summerbee. Or, as we call him, Bob the Slob.

> **TEDDY** *giggles;* **BOB**, *his mouth full, glares at* **JIMMY** *as surreptitiously as he can.*

ROSE: Clever name, First & Last. (To BOB.) Was it your idea?

BOB: No.

JIMMY: What you got there, Teddy?

TEDDY: My stamp album.

ROSE: The gentlemen don't wish to see that.

JIMMY: 'Course we do. Put it on the table, young man. I used to collect stamps. I've probably got a few Russian and French stamps you could have.

TEDDY: Don't want them.

JIMMY: Ah.

ROSE: *(Quickly.)* He only collects British Empire stamps, don't you, Teddy?

TEDDY: You know what they are?

JIMMY: Just about. I could probably find you some Canadian stamps.

TEDDY: Boring.

ROSE: (even more quickly.) He particularly likes the island stamps. Like the Pitcairn Islands. What other ones are there?

TEDDY: Trinidad and Tobago. St. Lucia. The Turks and Caicos Islands.

JIMMY: Because?

TEDDY: Because they're colourful.

ROSE: Yes, he likes colourful things, don't you, Teddy?

TEDDY: Do I?

ROSE: Yes, you do, you've got all your tropical birds. *(As if by explanation.)* These are Wills' cigarette cards.

TEDDY: But I'm still short of one. A Singhalese parrot.

JIMMY: Well, we'll see if we can capture it.

TEDDY: Do you smoke then?

JIMMY: I do on occasions. Not that brand. I'm a Turf man. But I know a Wills lady.

TEDDY: Gor, be smashing if you could find one. Do you wanna see the rest of the set?

ROSE: *(Firmly.)* No, no, not now. Another time. The gentlemen have been travelling, Teddy. And it's "want to" not "wanna".

TEDDY: Crewe's not far.

ROSE: They met up at Crewe. Mr. Last has come up today all the way from our capital city, the centre of the empire, and Mr. First has struggled to get here from Barnsley.

> **BOB,** *who hasn't appeared particularly interested in this conversation, pushes his empty plate away.*

BOB: Well, that's stopped the dog barking, Mrs Hoskins.

ROSE: That's what I like to see. And there's still some left for your main meal tomorrow. Now, Teddy, off to bed please.

TEDDY: Is yours a funny act?

BOB: *(Not a laugh.)* Ha, ha, ha. We don't know yet, flower.

JIMMY: We're still…um, thrashing it out. I think we've got a good beginning and Bob here seems to think we've got a good middle…

BOB: …which is why we've come up a couple of days early…

JIMMY: …to look around for an ending.

ROSE: I thought you were top of the bill.

BOB: Well, it's not so much that we're top of the bill, it's that there's nowt much below us.

JIMMY: It's…summer variety.

TEDDY: I love variety. The comic who stayed with us last year used to say "Life is the spice of variety." I thought that was very funny every single time he said it.

JIMMY: Then we'll have to get you a ticket to come and see us.

TEDDY: Mum says we can go three times as there are three changes of programme.

ROSE: *(Embarrassed.)* We do tend to see every show our guests are in. They're very generous with tickets. Right, off you go.

TEDDY: I like Eddie & Freddie.

BOB: Oh gawd. Have they played here?

TEDDY: No, I've heard them on my wireless.

JIMMY: You've got your own wireless?

ROSE: A crystal set. He makes them. He may not be able to walk as fast as an ostrich but he's a wizard with electricity. Aren't you, Teddy?

TEDDY: Do you wanna come and hear?

ROSE: They do not! Now, go to bed! These gentlemen need their sleep – as do you. They've got funny lines to think up in the morning.

TEDDY: *(Standing his ground.)* What you need is an onion at the end. Have you got one?

BOB: How d'you know about that?

TEDDY: I know about a lot of fings. I hear a lot. In there. I talk to the guests. They tell me all sorts of fings.

ROSE: Things, Teddy, things.

TEDDY: 'Ave you?

ROSE: Have you. He's very tired.

BOB: No, actually, we 'aven't.

JIMMY: But it's a very good idea, young man.

ROSE: Please, what is this onion?

BOB: It's…how can I put it?…it's…

TEDDY: …it's a song or it could be a story…couldn't it?…or a recitation or anyfing really that you put in at the end of your act to make the audience go all tearful. I'm right, aren't I?

JIMMY: Yeah, you are. Top marks, Teddy. 'Course, you don't want the punters getting too upset, just a little bit emotional I'd say – enough to remind them of what they're trying to forget – and then when you've got them feeling just sentimental enough you hit them with your play-off music.

ROSE: I thought you were supposed to make 'em laugh.

TEDDY: You've got to give 'em a bit of variety, mum.

ROSE: Yes, and if you're not careful I'll be giving you a bit of variety where you can really feel it. Now off to bed and leave us in peace or there'll be an onion at the end of this very evening.

> **TEDDY** *turns tail and heads to his room. At the door he stops and turns and looks about to speak again.*

I mean it.

> *(He goes.)*

He has dreams of being a stage manager you know. But he's never going to be one, poor love.

JIMMY: He's a little character though.

ROSE: Yes, he's my little sunshine, that's what. He's just so…chirpy. Like his birds. Now, the tea. I keep forgetting.

> *(She heads off to the kitchen.)*

Remind me. What's the show called?

BOB: "Follies on Parade."

ROSE: *(Off.)* Ooh, yes, I like that. And how many spots have you got?

BOB: Two. One in each half.

ROSE: *(Off.)* And you've written the beginning and the middle of both spots or one of them?

BOB: Just the second. We've left the first till last, haven't we, Last?

JIMMY: Yes, First.

ROSE: *(Off.)* Sounds to me like you've got your work cut out.

BOB: We'll get there.

> **ROSE** *appears in the doorway.*

ROSE: I need the deposit for the whole season you know, not just for the first show.

JIMMY: Don't worry yourself, Mrs Hoskins. We'll be a smash hit.

ROSE: Well, I hope so – but everyone in the lavatory told me that.

She disappears from sight again. The men look at each other dolefully.

Quick fade of lights.

SCENE THREE

Lights remain at black. Short montage of sounds from a seaside resort in summer, including the buzz and babble from a beach on a sunny day topped by the sporadic screams of excited children, the gentle breaking and lapping of waves, a silver band in full tune on a bandstand, the communal screams of children reacting to a Punch & Judy show, the clicks and clunks and beeps from an amusement arcade, bursts of laughter from a seaside show, barkers advertising boat and donkey rides, etc.

These sounds fade out as lights go up on the dress circle bar in the Winter Gardens, Southport. Posters of previous shows cover the red, flock wallpaper. It is a hot day. The windows are open and the sound of sea meeting the shore drifts in. N.B. If budgets do not permit, it would be possible to play this scene on the forestage in front of the tabs.

JIMMY *and* **BOB** *have improvised a stage.*

BOB: …oh, it's a sad world, it really is. I saw a boy coming out of the undertaker's crying. I said, "Why are you crying?" And he said –

JIMMY: Hey, what you messing about at?

BOB: What d'you mean?

JIMMY: Feeding yourself. That's what I'm here for.

BOB: You said you didn't like being the straight man.

JIMMY: I don't, matey. But I don't care for being made redundant either.

BOB: Okay. Let's try again. I saw a boy coming out of the undertaker's crying.

JIMMY: Oh dear. And did you give him a comforting word?

BOB: I did. I said, "Why are you crying?"

JIMMY: And what did he say to that?

BOB: What did he say to that? He said, "The undertaker hit me."

JIMMY: No!

BOB: What he said. So I went inside quick as a flash and said "Did you hit this little boy?"

JIMMY: Quite right.

BOB: And he said, "Yes, and I'll hit him again if he comes in asking for empty boxes."

JIMMY: Speaking of empty boxes, Mr. First, the other day --

> **DILLY** *enters carrying some sheet music. It should be clear in the Southport scenes that, being a soubrette now, she has come up in the theatrical world and is therefore more demurely dressed than when she was a chorus girl. But this is only comparatively speaking.*

DILLY: It's only little me.

BOB: Oh, hello, Dilly.

DILLY: Don't stop on my account.

JIMMY: You're in early.

DILLY: Yes, I got up early. Couldn't sleep much.

JIMMY: I can see.

DILLY: What d'you mean?

JIMMY: You look like you've been tied to the bedposts all night.

DILLY: Charming!

BOB: Don't bother with him, Dill. I'm your man.

DILLY: If it was pick-up-able, I wouldn't touch either of you with the greasy pole from the regatta.

JIMMY: We don't mean it, Dilly.

DILLY: No, nor do I, I was just sparing your feelings.

BOB: We'll have to transfer our affections elsewhere then, Jim.

JIMMY: Got a new song?

DILLY: I have.

JIMMY: Like me to play it through for you?

DILLY: No, I'd rather have it up to speed. (Of the sheet music.) Thought I'd get it on the piano and stake my claim.

BOB: Just think, Dill, one day you'll have top billing and you'll be able to strut in here and have first rehearsal whoever's got their music down ahead of you.

DILLY: Ooh, I pray for the day. So why are you two in so early?

JIMMY: We're been called. By the Supreme Being. By the Maker of All Things on the cheap.

DILLY: Oh…him.

BOB: Whose train gets in at eleven.

DILLY: Right…

JIMMY: We just thought we'd get in a quick run through of the routine that's not quite working.

DILLY: Which one is this?

JIMMY: Ooh, isn't she quick?

DILLY: I hope you've got more for me in the next show.

JIMMY: We will, we will.

DILLY: You owe me, you know.

BOB: We know. We're very grateful.

DILLY: Anyway, I've got news for you boys. I…I'm sure I saw Mr. Sandford down by the stage door five minutes ago.

BOB: Oh, bleedin' heck, we'd better get on.

DILLY: *(Innocent.)* Why's he called you?

BOB: Dunno.

JIMMY: He's down for the matinee apparently. Probably wants to put his oar in somewhere.

DILLY: He is the producer.

JIMMY: Yes, and he's been there and done it all before, or so he tells us.

DILLY: Look, you can't say he doesn't know his onions.

JIMMY: Yeah, but what he doesn't tell us, as a little bird told me recently, is that when he was a comic he needed a bottle of whisky to get himself on stage every night.

DILLY: Well, I bet you'd like a warm up act to get you bigger laughs when you come on. Now, I must be toddling.

BOB: You coming down to the beach today, flower?

DILLY: No, I'm giving my swimsuit a wash. Then I'm seeing a friend over at the Queen's Arms. (*She makes to go.*) Oh, by the way, I've got you that parrot. (*She searches in her purse.*) I opened a packet last night and there it was peering at me.

JIMMY: Didn't it speak?

DILLY: (*Putting the cigarette card in front of* **JIMMY**'s *face.*) Yes, it said "Who's a pretty arsehole then" – if you'll pardon the pun.

> *She gives him the cigarette card.*

See you.

> *She goes.*

JIMMY: (*Lamely.*) Thanks, Dilly. It is very beautiful bird, look.

BOB: Christ, we haven't got time to looking at bloody parrots!

> **JIMMY** *pulls a face and slips the card in his pocket.*

We've got laughs to find. Now, come on. From the top.

> *They both exit.* **JIMMY** *immediately re-enters.*

JIMMY: (*To the audience.*) Why is it I'm always here first when my name's Last? I'll tell you what, while we're waiting I shall edify you with a short recitation from Alfred, Lord Tennyson's great masterpiece The Charge of the Light Brigade. Or, as he subtitled it, A Shilling in the Meter Will Avoid a Power Cut. Now, are you all sitting comfy?

> **BOB** *enters.*

Oh, there you are! You're looking smartly turned out.

BOB: I know. I got a bit blotto at the party last night.

JIMMY: What on earth's that to do with anything?

BOB: I was smartly turned out.

JIMMY: Why are you late?

BOB: I've been looking at the chorus girls' dressing room.

JIMMY: Oh have you?

BOB: There was a fire in there earlier.

JIMMY: Was it serious?

BOB: Well, it took five hours to put it out.

JIMMY: Five hours?

BOB: Aye! One hour to put the fire out and four hours to get the firemen out!

JIMMY: Well, it's not much of a job, is it? You need a perk or two.

BOB: Not much of a job. I know a man who never did a day's work in his life.

JIMMY: Never did a day's work?

BOB: A nightwatchman.

> **DANIEL SANDFORD** *enters. He is not smoking a cigar but he walks bent slightly backwards as if he is. A large man in his early fifties, he is gruff and bluff and unsurprisingly does not tolerate fools – or comedians – gladly. He is a Liverpudlian. He stands watching, unseen by them.*

I hear you've left that job you got last week – is that so?

JIMMY: I have.

BOB: Wasn't your boss surprised when he heard you were leaving?

JIMMY: No, he knew before I did! Hey, I get a laugh.

BOB: No, no, we need to cut that. That's not been working. Look, let's skip that section and go straight to the next one. Go on, you'll get a laugh here. So…patter, patter, patter *and…*

JIMMY: …well, my wife is getting so thin that if she drinks a glass of bubbly they think she's a spirit level.

BOB: You're the lucky one. Someone mistook my house for a coast guard station last night.

JIMMY: In what way?

BOB: Some chap rang us seven times to ask the wife if the coast was clear.

> **DAN** *steps forward.*

JIMMY: Well, you'll never believe it, but the neighbours have made a collection to send my wife to --

DAN: *(Overlapping.)* The trouble with this routine…

BOB: Oh, hello, Mr. Sandford.

DAN: …is the punch line.

JIMMY: We haven't got there yet.

DAN: I saw the act last night.

BOB: But I thought you were coming down later this –

DAN: Caught the second half.

JIMMY: Why didn't you come round after?

DAN: I had work to do. Back at the Queen's Arms. Last minute change of plans.

BOB: And what did you think of the show?

DAN: Not bad. Not bad at all. But the second programme will be better value.

JIMMY: Are you directing it, Mr. Sandford?

DAN: I am. And as I was saying, punch lines will be punch lines. You know, whenever anyone sends me a sketch, I always read the punch line first. If I like it, I read the whole sketch from the beginning. If I don't, it's in the basket. If you get me.

BOB: So how are you keeping, Guv?

> **DAN** *looks for, finds and sits in the nearest chair as he speaks.*

DAN: Oh, I'm fine, I'm fine. I'll tell you, I was out on the front just a minute ago watching a dog crap on the promenade, and I thought, you know, I'm lucky I've never felt the need for a dog all my life. And yesterday, when I was coming over on the train, I also felt a very lucky man when I realized that no one's ever offered to give up a seat for me on a bus or a train. Now, don't you think that's a sign of good health?

BOB: You're a piece of Southport rock, Guv'nor, with Epsom Salts written through the middle.

DAN: Got to be. There are dozens and dozens of folks depending on me. Which is why I asked to see you…

BOB: Is there a problem?

DAN: There is, Bob, there is. Cos you see…I've had a worrying report.

JIMMY: Who from?

DAN: Our long suffering stage manager.

JIMMY: What's he been saying?

DAN: You're not up to standard, lads. (Silencing an impending protest with his hand before it can begin.) Which I just couldn't believe – until I saw the box office returns…

BOB: It's been really nice weather for this early in the summer. People have been staying on beach.

DAN: …but more, until I saw it with my very own eyes.

> *(He gets up and moves away.)*

I mean, fair enough, I didn't see the first half, but of what I did see I thought you were more 3rd rate than 1st rate, Mr. First, and you, Mr. Last, were very appropriately named.

(The men begin to protest aloud this time. **DAN** ploughs on.)

And as for the onion at the end, it was, in truth, the only truly risible part of the act! Yes, it brought tears to my eyes, but tears of laughter I'm sorry to say. It's no good serving up fake sentimentality, gentlemen. You've got to mean to tug at the heart strings. But not too hard mind you. *(Chuckling.)* We don't want to make it too real, do we now?

BOB: But this is only the first show of the summer. We've two more.

DAN: Exactly. We've three more months here and your jalopy's already running on empty.

JIMMY: *(Flabbergasted.)* But…I just don't get this…

DAN: …well, I do. Let's put it like this. Variety, as I see it, is really just a collection of cottage industries. And yours is going bust because you're not supplying it with any electricity. Of course, I should have followed my instinct. I just knew in my bones that it's not possible to put a Northerner and a Southerner together.

JIMMY: So, are you saying we're not doing anything well?

BOB: Aye, are we not even fitting in okay with the production numbers?

DAN: You are there, yes, because I produced 'em. I've been out there, boys. I know what I'm doing.

BOB: So…you think we're up to scratch when we're with the *rest* of the company but…?

DAN: He's good. You'll do. But we're not talking song and dance here, we're talking *(He snaps his fingers.)* laugh *(He snaps his fingers again.)* laugh *(and again.)* laugh. And what are we getting?

> *(He snaps his fingers three more times, leaving an unpleasant gap between snaps.)*

JIMMY: *(After a beat.)* It's not quite as bad as that, Mr. Sandford.

DAN: No, but it might as well be for all the good you'll do to my takings for the rest of the summer. You told me you'd worked together before.

BOB: We have.

DAN: No you haven't.

BOB: At the Derbyshire Miners' Camp in Skegness.

DAN: No you didn't.

JIMMY: We did.

DAN: I've checked.

BOB: Ah...

DAN: So, as you might gather, I am not best pleased with you lads in this moment of time. On the other hand, and I'm bending over backwards to be fair here, I have heard from a member of the company – via the stage manager – that you have a lot of potential...

BOB: Oh, that's nice.

JIMMY: Who was this?

DAN: Never you mind. Unfortunately, I have no interest in potential. I'm not in this business to bring on the next generation of stars – who'll all sod off to radio or the pictures or some island in the Mediterranean. I want my money's worth NOW.

JIMMY: We're getting there, Mr. Sandford.

DAN: No you're not. You're just getting in each other's way. (To BOB.) You can't sing, so why stick your nose in there. (To JIMMY.) And you're the feed. So why are you trying to get laughs?

BOB: I've said that to him.

JIMMY: You can't talk, you kept on and on asking me to write you a song, and then when I did --

BOB: A song does have to have a tune you know, or --

JIMMY: If you weren't tone deaf it --

DAN: Now, now, now, that's enough! This is the problem in a nutshell. I don't care whether you two see eye to eye. That means nothing in this business. Look at Abbott and Costello. They hate each other's guts.

BOB: I wouldn't say we hate each other. There's no reason. We're just don't click with one another, do we, Jim?

JIMMY: Clickety-click. No we don't.

DAN: Look, who's bloody interested! What matters is that you're not delivering the soddin' goods. And that's because you and you are putting your own petty needs to feel big about yourself before the punters need to have good night out. And I will not have it in my theatre.

Silence.

BOB: I'm sure we can...put together something that's...that's tip-top for the next show.

DAN: I don't think you're hearing what I'm saying here. We're in the middle of a Depression. Maybe not in Southport, but back in Liverpool there are people who are walking around without any shoes on their feet. People everywhere going hungry. When the punters walk through those foyer doors they haven't come to have their brains taxed. They deserve to have their lives brightened up not plunged into bloody darkness.

JIMMY: But the act's got a few real belters in it.

DAN: I'm not talking about your material! Your writing's fine. Punch lines aside, it's not your gags, it's your timing I'm worried about. You look like two amateurs up there. Like it's talent contest time. Now I know you're both pros. And though I didn't direct it, I thought you were both smack on the money in *Sinbad* back at the Argyll – otherwise you wouldn't be here. So something's not gelling. And I haven't got time to wait for it to set.

BOB: So what are you suggesting?

DAN: That you get your cards.

Silence.

BOB: And what would you do without us? The posters are already up for the second programme.

DAN: Well, put it like this. Eddie & Freddie have finished their radio season. And I don't bear them too many grudges.

JIMMY: You're kidding us, aren't you, Mr. Sandford?

DAN: Look, boys, I've got my wife to think of, and my daughter – who's just come back home with her suitcase -- and my box office staff, and my stage management and -- who else? – oh yes, of course, my artists. It's a tight ship I have to run. And as you know, we don't do tat. In this empire we offer the highest standard of entertainment that can be achieved on a budget.

BOB: Well, that's us. Cheap laughs!

DAN: Firing a person – or persons – is not a laughing matter in my book.

JIMMY: But we have a contract.

DAN: So? I'd pay you to stand in the wings if I had to. What would that do to your careers? In any case, did you have a contract for that sketch you used for your audition? Don't look so innocent. I mean the one you nicked from Chalk & Cheese.

BOB: *(After a beat.)* How did you find out about that?

DAN: Little bird told me.

JIMMY: There seems to be a flock of 'em.

DAN: And what's that supposed to mean?

JIMMY: Oh, nothing.

DAN: You must have meant something.

JIMMY: It really doesn't matter.

DAN: No, I don't suppose it does really. (Pause.) Right now, I must go. Don't you find there's always something else to do other than what you're actually doing? I do.

> *He turns to go.*

BOB: Please, Mr. Sandford, please.

> **DAN** *stops and turns.*

Give us a second chance.

DAN: I gave you that in rehearsals.

BOB: A final chance then.

DAD: Why should I?

JIMMY: We'll never get another booking mid season.

DAN: That's not my problem, young man. You'll just have to wait till the pantomime season, and then perhaps you could try out somewhere else for the Ugly Sisters – (pointedly.) or the Two Robbers.

BOB: There's no copyright on routines, Mr. Sandford.

DAN: How would you like it if yours were stolen? I've got my reputation to think of, Mr. Summerbee. I've employed the best in the country and I'm proud to say I still retain their respect. My artists may not all like me, but believe it or not they know where they stand with me. I'm not saying I'm as honest as the day is long, as there are some very long days in the theatre. But I do my best.

BOB: All right, maybe we didn't put on such a good show last night. But it's gone better.

DAN: Must have done. (*Going.*) I'll pay you till the end of the week.

JIMMY: I'm sure there're members of the company who'll vouch for us.

DAN: What, like the jugglers?

JIMMY: Like the M.D., like Michael Magic…like Dilly…

    DAN *stops in his tracks.* **JIMMY** *continues quickly.*

I bet she'd put in a word on our behalf. If you were to ask her…

DAN: Dilys is a soubrette, what does she know?

BOB: She's very special.

DAN: Yes, she's got spark that girl. And you're wasting her.

JIMMY: We could write her a bespoke sketch.

DAN: Oh, could you now?

BOB: Oh, aye, we could create one that fitted her like a glove.

DAN: No…I don't think so. Eddie & Freddie can do that.

JIMMY: Well, I heard them back at the digs on the radio recently, and I have to say I think our material's better.

DAN: Oh, do you?

JIMMY: I do.

DAN: But not your punch lines.

JIMMY: Perhaps not those.

DAN: And especially not your teamwork. Am I right, or am I right?

    Silence. **DAN** *ponders the problem for a moment until a thought appears to strike him.*

I'll tell you what. I will give you one last chance…

BOB: …oh, thanks, Guv'nor…

DAN: …on one condition. Take it or leave it.

JIMMY: I think we might take it.

DAN: Wait till you've heard. Yes, I think this is just what you need. My condition – are you listening? -- is that you talk in rhyme.

JIMMY: What?

BOB: Say that again.

DAN: All the time.

BOB: You mean…as long as we put our routines in rhyme, not just the onion at the end…you'll let us…?

DAN: An onion at the end doesn't have to be in rhyme. And your routines definitely don't.

BOB: I'm sorry, Guv'nor, I'm completely at a loss here…what do we put in rhyme then?

DAN: Everything else you say.

BOB: What, when we're around the theatre?

DAN: Whenever you're in each other's company.

BOB: But…we're sharing the same bloody digs! **JIMMY:** Are you really serious?

DAN: Oh, I'm serious all right. I'm a serious man, you see. And I seriously want a good show. And the only way you'll give it me is to be more in tune. To think as one. To think faster. To be snappier. And generally, to improve your bloody timing.

JIMMY: Sorry, I'm just not getting this. You're asking us to talk in rhyme… where? On the beach? In our digs? With the landlord at the pub?

DAN: You've got it in one.

JIMMY: But he can hardly talk in English, let alone in rhyme.

DAN: That's not what I'm saying. Who you lodging with?

BOB: A Mrs Hoskins.

DAN: Oh, Rose. She's famous. Well then, when you, Bob, are on your own with her – which may not necessarily be a wise thing to do – *you don't talk in rhyme. (To* **JIMMY**.*)* And the same applies. But when you're both with her or both in pub or both at the lido or both happily striding along the pier say, you do. You look puzzled.

JIMMY: I am because…I don't believe this…I mean, you're actually *ordering us* to talk in verse?

DAN: You could put it like that, yes. As I said, take it or leave it.

JIMMY: *(Dry.)* How many stresses would you require in every line?

DAN: I don't mind! Mix it up. That'll help speed up your reactions.

BOB: Sometimes I think I'm too fast for him.

DAN: Sometimes you are. But first and last, I'm hoping you'll stop squabbling and work as a team. I mean, communicate with each other for God's sake! One thing more though. It's rhyme that's needed here. Under no circumstance do we need any bloody poetry anywhere near the seaside. Do you hear me?

JIMMY: And what if we just say 'sod off', turn tail and walk out of here? What'll you do about the shows today?

DAN: *(A muted threat.)* Oh, you're thinking of giving up the business, are you?

BOB: And…how long would you require us to do this?

DAN: For as long as it takes. *(Pause.)* So do we have an agreement?

> Long pause, during which **JIMMY** and **BOB** exchange glances and even gestures.

JIMMY: We'll have to.

DAN: You will. And if I ever hear from the stage manager or anyone that one or other of you have reneged on this agreement, I'll just employ the one that didn't. And if you both do, we're back to where we were a few minutes ago, except that I'll be half-way to my hotel.

JIMMY: Ah, but we could do a deal with each other not to talk in rhyme when we're on our own. How would you know about that?

DAN: Do you trust each other that much?

> Silence.

Right, so, we'll get going shall we?

BOB: *(Picking up his coat.)* You still staying for the show, Guv'nor?

DAN: I meant, we'll get this rhyming up and running. Like, from here on. Ask me that again.

> **BOB** and **JIMMY** look at one another. **JIMMY** gestures for **BOB** to start. **BOB** gestures for **JIMMY** to start. **JIMMY** gestures again.)

I don't want you miming/ I want you rhyming! Don't you get it?

JIMMY: It was your question, Mr. First.

BOB: Oh, great. Right. Are you staying to see the Follies?/ Or will you be eating lollies/ On the train/ As you go home again/ To Liverpool/…and…walk past your old school?

DAN: *(After a beat.)* Why don't we try again?

BOB: Am I right in asking/ That you'll be basking/ On the sands this afternoon?/ Or will you be in stitches/ At the hitches/ In the show?/ Or come out humming…the toons?

DAN: I thought you were going to make it over the finishing line for a moment. It's a start though. Brave attempt at least. *(To* **JIMMY**.*)* Your turn. *(To* **BOB**.*)* But to answer your question, I'm back to Queen's Arms now – just…just for a quick bite – and then I'm heading off after the first half.

JIMMY: And at what time will we be rehearsing/ The show that you'll be nursing/ To success?/ And might we hope for a notice this time in the press?

DAN: No need to be funny. I've telephoned the editor and he assures me it won't happen again – or there'll be no tickets for that family.

JIMMY: So how was that?

DAN: Not bad at all.

BOB: It's easier for him. He writes songs.

DAN: B'time I'm done with you you'll be writing fucking operettas. So now, instead of rhyming on your own, you've got to rhyme back and forth. But I can't wait for that. My appetite's getting the better of me. And I have a feeling that, to start with, it's going to be pitiful. And I don't do pitiful. So ten o'clock Monday it is.

(He makes to go.)

BOB: We'll be there, bright and breezy/ *(He looks to* **JIMMY**.*)*

JIMMY: I'll be chalky, he'll be cheesy/ *(He looks to* **BOB**.*)*

BOB: Brimming with material/

JIMMY: That's not ethereal.

DAN: Yes, well, you've a long way to go, boys.

JIMMY: You say you want us to communicate, yet you throw up a bloody great barrier between us.

DAN: My old school – not the one near the station – taught me that barriers were for climbing. And there were sweet shops on the other side.

(He grins and exits.)

JIMMY: Now this really is the pits, don't you think?/

BOB: I think that it stinks/

JIMMY: The man is off his trolley/

BOB: You can be if you've got the lolly/

JIMMY: But how dare he? It's…it's…it's slavery/

BOB: Well, it's certainly unsavoury/

JIMMY: He's a tower of shit/

BOB: Ah, you've put your finger on it!/ And his tummy's not rumbling/ He wants to go fumbling/ Dilly

JIMMY: The dirty old sod/

BOB: You're peas in a pod/

JIMMY: Don't be silly.

(He picks up his script and other belongings.)

BOB: Then who has caught your eye?/

JIMMY: Well, after what Sandford said about Rose/ I'm thinking I might give her a try/

BOB: Are you staking a claim?/

JIMMY: No I'm claiming a steak I suppose/

BOB: Are we not meant to make sense?/

JIMMY: I sense that you're tense/

BOB: You're not joking/

JIMMY: I'm...I'm...well, I'm sick as a parrot/

BOB: Oh, the Singhalese parrot that swallowed a carrot?/

JIMMY: Mmm...and was found choking In Woking.

(**BOB** *grimaces*, **JIMMY** *holds his head in his hands.*)

BOB: Oh dear oh dear. How *did* we get here? How *did* we get into this fine mess?

(*Quick fade of lights.*)

SCENE FOUR

The parlour of the lodging house. It is late morning and seagulls can be heard occasionally and faintly.

TEDDY *comes out of the kitchen with a glass of milk and a spoon. He sits at the table and appears to be spooning the milk into his mouth. He makes quite a production of it.*

A door is heard to close and **JIMMY** *enters from the hall, carrying a newspaper under his arm. He is casually dressed.* **TEDDY** *rises guiltily.*

JIMMY: Don't get up on my account, son. (*After a glance up the stairs.*) Lovely day outside.

TEDDY: Lovely day inside.

JIMMY: Yeah, what you up to?

TEDDY: I was eating the top off the milk.

JIMMY: Does your mother know you're pinching the skin?

TEDDY: No, she's gone for her Sunday Guinness.

JIMMY: 'Cos mine would have known.

He sits in the armchair and idly glances through the newspaper as.

There were three of us boys and we all hankered after it. But you don't have any competition. Why can't you have it all to yourself?

TEDDY: It was promised to Mr. First for his pudding.

JIMMY: Oh blow him. I'll tell your mother I had it on my cornflakes.

TEDDY: Oh, fank'ou, Mr. Last.

JIMMY: Would that all milk had to be boiled all year round and we could have skin on everything we eat for ever.

TEDDY: Mum says she's saving for a refrigerator.

JIMMY: You mean she's not stopping at an inside lavatory?

TEDDY *giggles.* **JIMMY** *gets involved in a news item.* **TEDDY** *comes behind him and peers over his shoulder enough, eventually, to disturb him.*

Do you read the newspapers, Teddy?

TEDDY: No.

JIMMY: What's so interesting then?

TEDDY: That cartoon. (*He points at it and chortles.*) When you've finished with the paper I'll cut it out.

JIMMY: Will you now?

TEDDY: Yes. All the guests let me have their papers.

JIMMY: And what will you do with it after you've cut it out?

TEDDY: I'll stick it with the others in my scrapbook. I've got 'undreds.

JIMMY: You save a lot of things, don't you, Teddy?

TEDDY: Yes. Mum says I don't need a savings account.

JIMMY: I'm sure you don't. I save magnets. I've a drawer full of them back in Clapham.

TEDDY: What's special about magnets?

JIMMY: What's special about − ? Teddy, you should know that's not the kind of question you should ever ask a collector.

Pause. **JIMMY** *goes back to his newspaper.*

TEDDY: Mr. Last? Why aren't you rhyming this morning?

JIMMY: Because I don't have to when Bob's not around.

TEDDY: I like you rhyming.

JIMMY: You're in a minority of one then.

TEDDY: Will you do some rhyming for me? Before mum comes back.

JIMMY: No, I'm sorry, Teddy. I'm glad it gives you pleasure because it don't me. Don't ask again.

TEDDY *looks hurt but he soon bounces back.*

TEDDY: Would you like to buy a wireless set?

JIMMY: What, one of your cat's whisker jobbies?

TEDDY: Yeah, I'll make you one all for yourself.

JIMMY: I was quite happy listening to yours. And why would I need one? There's an Ekco AW 70 over there.

TEDDY: You could listen to it in your own room.

JIMMY: No, I don't think so, Teddy.

TEDDY: Keep up with the latest in radio comedy, Mr. Last.

JIMMY: I'm really…not --

TEDDY: *(Overlapping.)* I made one for Mrs Harris over in the blue house last week. I let her have it half price because she lets us use her telephone. She was very pleased with it. And the money helps mum out. Gives her a little extra. She −

JIMMY: *(Irritated.)* Oh, all right, yes, yes, you make me one.

TEDDY: You can have it half price if you do some rhyming for me.

JIMMY: Oh no, no, no, you little devil, Hobson's Choice it may be, but I'll pay the full whack.

He shuts his newspaper.

Nothing gets any better.

At this moment **BOB** *descends the stairs, yawning. He looks more than usually dishevelled.*

BOB: I was having a dream that I was rhyming/ Then I woke up and found I was climbing/ The walls, cos the nightmare's still with me/ Like having stones in me kidney…

> **TEDDY** *taps his fists together gleefully.*

Oh are you here, young Teddy?/

JIMMY: You said you'd be ready/ To rehearse this morning/ And here you are yawning/ At noon/

BOB: Well that's a nice greeting!/ You must have been eating/ Some prunes/

JIMMY: So why are you late?/

BOB: It was something I ate/

JIMMY: You mean drank.

BOB: It's true I succumbed/ I went to every bar bar one/ And got tanked/ But I can skip breakfast/ In fact, as it doesn't seem to rhyme with anything I'll give it a miss/

JIMMY: Which is just as well because Sandford, our nemesis/ Could appear at any juncture/ To see whether our rhyming's got a puncture/

BOB: Well, for God's sake let's get this show on the road/ Before I…I…I break out in an ode/

TEDDY: Can I watch?

BOB: We won't be top-notch/

TEDDY: Aww, I fink you're both really brilliant!

JIMMY: We're getting better it's true/ But it would be best if you withdrew/ As we might wish to shout at each other/

BOB: So where is your mother?

JIMMY: She's down at the hostelry.

BOB: Don't be awkward. It's hard enough as it is. Get in tune the Guv'nor said. Go on, try again.

JIMMY: She's gone to…her club/

BOB: You mean she's down at the pub/ So she'll come home and need to recover. Sorry about that, Teddy. That was just a rhyme. Didn't mean anything.

TEDDY: Don't mind. Let me stay and listen.

JIMMY: No!

TEDDY: Please!

JIMMY: You must be tireless/ And work on my wireless.

TEDDY: I'll do it later. Go on, let me.

JIMMY: I said –

TEDDY: I'm a good audience. I'm going to be a stage manager.

BOB: It's all right by me/ Come on, Jimmy, why can't he/ Sit there and see if we're funny?/ *(To* **TEDDY**.*)* Yes, sonny?

TEDDY: Yes, please.

JIMMY: But we're not testing out jokes/ About my piles or your bunion/ Because we said we would work on the onion.

BOB: Then why don't we try/ To make the boy cry?/

> *(Hold. He looks long and hard at* **JIMMY**. **JIMMY** *doesn't dissent.)*

You up for it, young fellow-me-lad?

TEDDY: Try me!

BOB: Okay, you're the stage manager, give us a stage…

> **TEDDY** *springs into action before they can change their minds, clearing some space and setting up some chairs as* **BOB** *waxes lyrical.*

Give us a stage/ And we'll show you an age/ Where mirth was the cousin of sadness/ Where gaiety was its mother/ And laughter its brother/ And granny…descended into madness.

> **TEDDY** *claps his fist together again.*

JIMMY: That'll do, that'll do. You sit on the carpet over there.

> **TEDDY** *obediently does so, but then immediately gets up.*

TEDDY: May I just go and find a handkerchief?

BOB: Oh, use your sleeve, I don't mind.

TEDDY: No, I mean, in case you make me too sad.

BOB: Are you trying to be funny?

TEDDY: I really ought to have a hankie ready. Just in case.

JIMMY: He's being sarcy.

TEDDY: *(Genuine.)* I'm not. I cry ever so easy.

BOB: Go on then, flower, make it quick.

> *(***TEDDY** *hurries off as quickly as he can manage.)*

I must say, this is a very long way from the Hollywood Hills!/

JIMMY: Yes, so far it's been all spills and not many thrills/

BOB: And what a way to spend our day off/

JIMMY: Not much of a pay off/

BOB: But then it's better than being down the mines/ Spending your life where the sun also doesn't shine.

JIMMY: I usually spend Sundays trying to trace my son/

BOB: *(After a beat.)* Did he, by chance, away from home run?/

He winces.

Sorry.

JIMMY: Away from home run he did not/ But the lady with whom I'd thrown in my lot/ Threw in hers and took him away/ With her lover I have to say/ And this without warning/ One November morning/

BOB *goes to speak.* **JIMMY** *holds up his hand.*

And sailed to Canada/ Which doesn't rhyme/ But in the fullness of time/ I received a postcard from Saskatchewan/ Which probably doesn't rhyme either…oh, yes it does…so you can see her plan/ She told me she wished to wash her hands of me/ And start a new life and I was never to see/ Them again. So, yes, I suppose I'm being a clown/ But on Sundays I write letters trying to track him down.

BOB: *(After a beat.)* Right. Let's get on. Teddy, hurry up!

TEDDY: *(Off.)* Coming.

TEDDY *re-enters with a box of handkerchiefs.*

Sorry. I was given some for Christmas but I couldn't find the box.

BOB: I suspect you won't need that many/

JIMMY: You might not need any/

BOB: Oh yes he will. I'll see to that. With a little song I have penned…

JIMMY: I didn't know you wrote songs, Mr. First.

BOB: This is my first, Mr Last. I'm becoming a blend/ To some people's annoyance/ Of talent and flamboyance.

He picks up **JIMMY**'s *ukulele and plays a chord.*

This is a little song entitled 'Your Auntie's Husband's Name is Robert', subtitled 'Bob's Your Uncle'. No, seriously, this is a heart-rending song I found one rainy day in the dustbin at the back of a workhouse.

He then pulls his top lip down over his teeth and adopts a croaky 'old man' voice.

You young fellows both have to go... (Sings.) pom-pom-pom- pom...when I nod my head. Okey-doke?

He starts strumming. After two bars he nods his head and the others join in the vamp until he begins singing in a manner a little too jaunty to match the sentiment of the words.

Why do you moan your life away?
Why are you full of groans?
Why do you feel so bitter at your age?
Wait till you get arthritis
Wait till you need a stick
Wait till you feel the icicles in your bones
Then you can moan
Then you can moan
Wait till you feel the icicles in your bones
I wish I had my time over again
I'd show you how to dance
I'd show you how to laugh
I'd show you life
I'd show you life
I'd show you life without a varicose vein

At the end of the chorus, **TEDDY** *claps his fists.*

This is sad, Teddy. Come on now, pom-pom-pom-pom... Both of you. Good.

(He sings the second verse, on his feet performing it this time.)

You've had the opportunities
You've seldom gone without
You've had the chance to do the things we dreamed
What have you got to pain you?
What have you got to hate?
What have you got to fight and cry about?
You can get out
You can get out
What have you got to fight and cry about?
I wish I had....*etc. to....*
....varicose vein *(finish.)*

Even before he has reached the end, **TEDDY** *has stuck the handkerchief in his mouth in an attempt to stop himself laughing.*

JIMMY: *(Of the ukulele.)* Give me that, give me that. Teddy! You're supposed to be tearful not cheerful.

TEDDY: I'm so sorry, Mr. First.

BOB: All right, clever clogs, you do better.

JIMMY: I will. I'll make those eyes a good deal wetter/ With my little operetta.

BOB: Which is called?

JIMMY: "She Sold Herself for an Onion, Now She's in a Awful Stew."

> **JIMMY** *now sings, in a considerably superior singing voice and with a more accomplished accompaniment.*

My old dad
Is ev'rything
A growing lad
Could wish for
Firm but kind
'e wouldn't mind
Were I to ask for more
Never gets angry or
Beats me or mum...
That's the dad
Yes, that's the dad
I wish I 'ad.

> **ROSE** *appears in the hall doorway unnoticed by the others and stands listening. She wears a more summery and revealing dress, and appears slightly the worse for wear.*

> **JIMMY** *has continued.*

My old dad
'e doesn't smoke
And doesn't bet
On greyhounds
Doesn't spend
His weekly wages
At the Rose & Crown
'e takes good care of me
Won't let me down...

That's the dad
Yes, that's the dad
I wish I 'ad.

> *At the end,* **TEDDY** *looks about to explode. To avoid doing so he scurries off into his room where he is heard to dissolve into fits of laughter.*

ROSE: Hey, what you done to the poor boy?

JIMMY: What has he done to us?

BOB: Lucky he's not hoping to become an undertaker.

JIMMY: Enjoy your Guinness, Rose?

ROSE: Oh, I did. A little too much I'm afraid. Let me sit down.

> *She sits at one end of the sofa.*

I must have had two, or was it three? What will you boys think of me? Now I'm doing it! I'm rhyming and you're not. But let's be thankful for small mercies, to coin a phrase. It was really getting on my nerves, you rhyming away in my parlour.

JIMMY: We haven't stopped. We just forgot.

BOB: We cannot relent/ If you're expecting the rent.

ROSE: But why don't you just spend your time apart?

JIMMY: Yes, that would be smart/ But there's work to be done/

BOB: And your puddings to be eaten/

JIMMY: Ah, I'm afraid you've been beaten/ To the skin off the milk/ I couldn't resist/ I was an opportunist/

BOB: I'll get you back/ I'll eat your next snack/

JIMMY: Then you'll get mustard in your custard!

ROSE: Boys, boys, this is getting really silly!

BOB: Sorry, Rose.

ROSE: Strikes me you could at least split up for the rest of the day.

JIMMY: *(To* **BOB**.*)* You going out at all?

BOB: No, I'm staying put. If you don't mind, Rose.

ROSE: No, no, I don't mind at all, Bob.

JIMMY: Then I'll go help Teddy/ With a job/ He's making me a receiver…/

ROSE: Ooh, I'm pleased to hear that.

JIMMY: So that I can hear news from Geneva.

ROSE: Oh really?

JIMMY: What do you think?

> *(He goes off into* **TEDDY**'s *room.)*

ROSE: He can be a rude man sometimes.

BOB: He certainly can.

ROSE: Loves the sound of his own voice, I'd say.

BOB: Well, he would. He's the Compliment Fishing Champion.

ROSE: And I really don't like him singing songs like that.

BOB: I didn't think it was too bad but don't go telling tell him I said so.

ROSE: I mean, Teddy's been asking questions about his father again and I don't like having to tell him fibs.

BOB: Tell him the truth then.

ROSE: What, that his father's paid good hush money so that he doesn't have to acknowledge him?

BOB: He's done…what? Who is he then?

ROSE: Oh, it doesn't matter. I'm talking far too much.

BOB: No, tell me. You've started now.

ROSE: *(Pointing to a photograph.)* Him. Here.

BOB: Good heavens above! But he's married.

ROSE: That's why he paid good money.

BOB: And famous.

ROSE: Very good money.

BOB: I mean, he's a genuine star. Got a wonderful voice.

ROSE: Who says he hasn't?

BOB: *(Incredulous.)* How did you meet him?

ROSE: I was in the business. Just started. In the chorus. My career began and ended all in a summer season.

BOB: What did you do with the money?

ROSE: You're surrounded by it.

> **BOB** *looks puzzled.*

I bought this house. Well, put down a sizable deposit. It would have ended his career if it had come out. Still could.

BOB: Does Jimmy know any of this?

ROSE: 'Course he doesn't know. We're not close, you know. Did you think we were?

BOB: No…

ROSE: I'm not saying I don't like him. Suppose I could get to like him. Because…he has been making suggestions, you know.

BOB: Oh has he?

ROSE: Not crude ones. Just showing an interest I suppose.

BOB: So it's not a bad thing to show an interest then?

ROSE: Depends who's showing it, Bob.

> **BOB** *sits at the other end of the sofa.*

BOB: Really?

> **ROSE** *immediately gets up and walks away.*

ROSE: What a relief! No rhyming for a bit. Ooh, I am a bit tiddly.

BOB: So, what did you mean, Rose?

ROSE: I think you know, Bob, I think you know.

BOB: Do I?

ROSE: Don't 'Do I?' me. I've seen signals.

BOB: Why don't you come and sit down?

ROSE: I would, but…Teddy's in there. He hears everything. That's why he knows so much about show business. He earwigs. The other day I found a wine glass in there next to the wall. Still, poor lad, he hasn't much else to do.

BOB: Will he get better?

ROSE: Well, there are always miracles. But the doctor tells me it's degenerative. Teddy doesn't know, of course.

BOB: He doesn't appear too bad at the moment.

ROSE: No it seems to go in phases. There's no predicting.

BOB: Can't be much fun for you.

ROSE: No… *(Making an effort.)* But we've got to enjoy whatever we can.

BOB: That's what I say. Come and sit over here.

ROSE: Well…just for a minute. Then I'll put on the potatoes.

> *(She sits back at her end of the sofa.* **BOB** *whispers to her.)*

I'm sorry, I missed that.

BOB: I'm whispering so that Teddy and Jimmy can't hear. If you come a bit nearer, I won't have to raise my voice.

    ROSE *wiggles her way along the sofa.*

Seems to me, Rosie, that you're in need of a cuddle.

ROSE: *(Also whispering.)* Mmm, I am. I really am.

BOB: And a kiss.

    She looks at him intently. He looks at her. They seem about to kiss, but at this moment **JIMMY** *enters.*

JIMMY: Oh, sorry...we're looking for the screwdriver.

    Blackout.

INTERVAL

ACT TWO

SCENE ONE

First & Last's dressing room in Southport. It looks much the same as their previous dressing room in Birkenhead but is slightly more glamorized. It is clearly nearer the stage, as those entering are not out of breath on arrival. At this moment the room is unoccupied.

There is a knock on the door. Then silence. Then another. After a suitable pause the dressing room door slowly opens.

DILLY: *(Off.)* It's only little me.

> **DILLY** *pops her head round the door, enters cautiously and looks around. She is costumed as a milkmaid ready for a night out.*

They're not here yet. Come in, they won't mind.

> **TEDDY** *enters, steered in by* **ROSE**.

Have you been back before?

ROSE: Well, yes…in the past. We love coming back, don't we, Teddy?

TEDDY: I like it better than the show.

ROSE: Well, that's nice! This young lady will think you didn't enjoy her bits.

TEDDY: No, I think she's got some smashing bits.

ROSE: Let's draw a veil over that one, shall we?

DILLY: *(Amused.)* I'm sure there's a drink for you somewhere.

ROSE: That would be nice.

DILLY: Though I'd better not go raiding their larder. They'll be here in a minute I'm sure. I'm Dilly by the way.

ROSE: I think we know! We saw you in the first show as well.

TEDDY: This one's better.

DILLY: Yes…I think we're getting into the swing of things now. And you are?

ROSE: I'm Rosemary. And this is young Teddy.

DILLY: Ah, yes, you must be the boys' landlady?

ROSE: How did you know?

DILLY: Mine came yesterday. Brought her grandfather. *(Aside to* **ROSE**.*)* Dirty old man.

> *(***ROSE*** *pulls a slightly amused, slightly disgusted face.* **TEDDY** *looks puzzled.)*

So, what would you like to be when you grow up, Teddy?

TEDDY: A stage manager.

DILLY: Really?

TEDDY: Oh yes. I want to work here. Could you get me a job?

DILLY: Well!

ROSE: Please, Teddy, please, please, please!

TEDDY: What?

ROSE: Give the lady a chance. And you're not old enough yet.

DILLY: Maybe we could find him a little job. Sweeping the stage on a Saturday morning. Or something like that.

TEDDY: Oh yes, fank you, that would be super.

ROSE: I think you mean 'thank you', don't you, Teddy?

DILLY: Well, I'll put out a few feelers.

ROSE: You really don't need to --

DILLY: So what did you think of the boys tonight?

ROSE: Very funny. Very funny indeed.

DILLY: You, Teddy?

TEDDY: I like the bit where they're pirates and Mr. First tries to do the splits and then says, 'Half tonight and half tomorrow night.'

DILLY: Mmm. And did you like the butter sketch?

TEDDY: The one you were in?

DILLY: Well, yes. My big moment in the second half.

TEDDY: Not bad. But I've a better idea.

ROSE: Oh, Teddy, for goodness sake!

DILLY: No, let him. Go on, what's better than the butter?

> *(She chuckles at her own little piece of word-play.* **ROSE** *feels obliged to join in.* **TEDDY** *is the picture of seriousness.)*

TEDDY: What I'm finking… *(His mother mouths 'thinking'.)* …is that… you're sitting on a wall singing *By the Light of the Silvery Moon*.

DILLY: *(She likes this idea.)* Ah.

TEDDY: Then Mr. Last pops up from behind the wall, sits next to you and joins in with you.

DILLY: (This is not quite such a good idea but acceptable.) Ah.

TEDDY: Then Mr. First pops up between you both, from behind, and pulls Mr. Last backwards off the wall – onto something soft that we can't see, of course – sits on the wall himself, and takes Mr. Last's place in the song.

DILLY: (This is not so good.) Ah.

TEDDY: Then Mr. Last pops back up again and pulls you off the wall.

DILLY: (This is beyond problematic.) Aaahhh!

TEDDY: And then he climbs on the wall and the song carries on with him and Mr. First.

DILLY: *(This is an especially bad idea.)* Mmmm.

TEDDY: Then you pop up between them and pull them both off the wall…

DILLY: *(Opens her mouth but no sound escapes.)*

TEDDY: …and get back on the wall and finish the song.

    (Pause.)

DILLY: Yes, yes… That's a very funny idea, Teddy. And I'm sure the *boys* would love all that tumbling about behind the set. But I really don't fancy going arse over head – if you'll pardon the pun – even if it's on to a feather mattress. Keep thinking though, you're on the right lines. Now I must go and get out of all this clobber.

    (She makes for the door. As she reaches it, **BOB** *and* **JIMMY** *appear.)*

Oh, they're here. You've got visitors.

BOB: Oh, how nice!/

JIMMY: Three blind mice!

    (General greetings between **BOB**, **JIMMY**, **ROSE** *and* **TEDDY**, *out of which we hear* **ROSE** *saying.)*

ROSE: …oh, it was wonderful!

BOB: Really?

ROSE: You were *so* funny. And you were too, Jimmy.

BOB: Coming on, is it?

ROSE: Oh, it's come, it's come.

JIMMY: And what about our Dilly?

ROSE: Major talent.

DILLY: Ooh…

BOB: *(In a cod West Country accent.)* Yep, we make good butter, don't we, gentle milkmaid?

DILLY: *(Ditto.)* We do kind farmer.

> *(All roar with laughter at what is now obviously an in joke.)*

BOB: Sorry we kept you waiting/ We've been berating/ The MD for killing a laugh in the pirate sketch/ The wretch.

JIMMY: We hit him over the head with his baton/ Now he can't get his hat on.

ROSE: It was no problem. Miss Williams kept us well entertained.

BOB: Thanks, Dill.

DILLY: That's all right. I was a cowgirl in the first half of the show, a milkmaid in the second and Bo Peep rescuing two lost sheep in the corridor afterwards. I'll be a pig-keeper next.

BOB: You deserve some imbibing fluid, my darling.

DILLY: Thought you'd never ask.

BOB: *(Sitting at his dressing table.)* Everyone else for a drink?

TEDDY: Not me, fank you.

> **BOB** *pulls* **ROSE** *onto his knee, much to* **JIMMY'S** *irritation,* **TEDDY'S** *embarrassment and* **DILLY'S** *amusement.*

BOB: Jimmy. You're nearest. Pour the ladies a snifter.

> **JIMMY** *looks further put out by this request but his social graces get the better of him and he pours drinks as.*

He's not fast/ But he's swifter/ Than Otto in the bar/ The one that likes the jolly jack tars.

ROSE: Now, now, Bob, not in front of Teddy. In any case, the man can't help his anomaly.

BOB: Sorry, my old peach.

> *(Though sitting on* **BOB'S** *knee,* **ROSE** *now sits up as primly as she can.)*

ROSE: So...what's coming up next?

DILLY: Sorry?

ROSE: What follies are you all going to be parading for the two of us?

DILLY: Oh, we'll find some.

ROSE: Do you do requests?

DILLY: I don't expect Mr. Sandford would take to that. We just tend to do what he tells us.

BOB: Mmm, well, the singers do, and the dancers/ But us comics have to come up with our own answers/ Still, I say let's forget what's coming/ And indulge ourselves in conduct unbecoming.

DILLY: *(Raising her glass.)* Here, here.

    JIMMY *hands* **BOB** *a drink.*

BOB: That's a bit stingy.

JIMMY: Half tonight and half tomorrow night.

    TEDDY *stifles a laugh. Without a smile on his face,* **JIMMY** *moves away, pours   himself a drink and begins changing as best he can in front of the women.*

ROSE: Everything okay, Jimmy?

JIMMY: Fine.

BOB: Jimmy's a bit miffed because he's doing such a fantastic job feeding me gags/

JIMMY: Because I feel like a builder's labourer who can't afford any fags/

DILLY: Fags! That reminds me. Did you get that parrot?

TEDDY: Oh, was it from you, miss? Yes, I did. Fank you, fank you, fank you. I've got it under my pillow at the moment.

ROSE: That pillow has lots of secrets, hasn't it, Teddy?

    TEDDY *nods.*

DILLY: I like secrets too, Teddy. I think everyone should have one. Anyone not got one?

    Silence.

ROSE: So...Jimmy, we all think you're a star.

DILLY: Here, here.

ROSE: In my humble opinion, the act's improved beyond all recognition.

DILLY: It's the rhyming that's done it.

BOB: Now, don't you start, my girl. It's an f-ing imposition, and that's the end of it.

DILLY: But it's working. You've got the knack. You're starting to gel.

BOB: Oh, turn it off!

ROSE: Well, I'm sorry, Bobbie, but I have to agree with Dilys.

BOB: And you can pipe down.

ROSE: Say what you like, but the way you two talk in rhyme – just like that – well, it sets you apart. It makes you –

JIMMY: I know you think we go together like pudding and suet/ But you're not the ones who have to do it/ We're the ones with egg on our faces/ We're the ones who feel we're wearing braces/ Outside our coats, who can't go to the races/ Because we'll stick out like sore thumbs/ So, please ladies, if you have any comfort, throw us some crumbs.

    DILLY, **ROSE** and **TEDDY** *applaud.*

DILLY: You see. You're thinking quicker.

BOB: *(Dry.)* Oh, well done, Jimmy.

ROSE: Yes, in my humble opinion Mr. Sandford's done you a favour.

BOB: Rose, will you get up please? My knee's about to give way.

    She does so, looking a little crushed.

JIMMY: The thing is, Dilly, this may sound perverse/ But when you're speaking in verse/ You don't know where you sentence is going/ And although to some it's amusing/ Though to others bemusing/ There isn't much fun in not knowing.

DILLY: Yes, but I don't expect there's much fun working on your scales if you're a proper singer – but apparently it makes the difference.

JIMMY: I didn't say we were going to stop/ We'd still like to get to the top/

BOB: I think what he's saying/ Is that it's better than bricklaying/ Or being a mechanic/ But it sets the ears steaming/ If you can't say what you're meaning/ As you tend to end up in a panic.

DILLY: But we understand you.

ROSE: Everyone understands you.

> **TEDDY** *suddenly holds up his hand and starts jumping up and down.*

TEDDY: I've got an idea, I've got an idea!

ROSE: Oh, Teddy, for heaven's sake! You said you'd behave! *(To the others.)* Sorry, but we must be toddling along.

DILLY: Oh, Rose, let him. We don't mind. It's for their act, is it, Teddy?

TEDDY: Yes. I fink they should do it in rhyme.

> *General disagreement.*

I don't mean, no…I don't mean they shouldn't do routines and songs and onions and things…

BOB: By the way, what did you think of the onion tonight, Teddy?

TEDDY: It didn't make me laugh.

BOB: Aye, but did it make you wet-eyed?

TEDDY: No, but it made me foughtful.

JIMMY: Well, that's a start I suppose.

DILLY: So what's this idea, Teddy?

TEDDY: I fink you should talk to the audience in rhyme *in between* the songs and sketches and dances.

BOB: What, encourage them to heckle us?

TEDDY: Get them to suggest subjects, like a memory man does, then when they say fings or call out, you rhyme with what they say.

> *Silence.*

DILLY: I think that's a brilliant idea.

ROSE: So do I.

BOB: Well I don't.

JIMMY: Nor me.

DILLY: But it'd be really different, boys.

BOB: No, no, no, no, no.

> *Together.*

JIMMY: Absolutely not.

BOB: We want out/ We don't want in/

JIMMY: We want stout/ We don't want gin.

All look at **JIMMY** *for enlightenment. He shrugs.*

BOB: Sorry, Teddy.

JIMMY: Yeah, sorry, son, but one of our aims/ Is to be set free of all this, not tied up in more chains.

DILLY: But listen, listen to me! I'm sure, if he sees his idea working before his very eyes, Mr. Sandford will be more inclined to let you off the hook.

ROSE: She's got a point, Bobsey.

DILLY: And besides that, if you could pull it off, it could make your fortune.

ROSE: Oh yes, make you stand out from the rest. Top of the bill material I'd say. Proper top.

DILLY: Palladium material.

TEDDY: Radio material I fink.

Another silence.

BOB: *(A new tone has come into his voice.)* But...the Guv'nor would go nuts if we changed the act/

JIMMY: He's right, it's a fact./ Or bananas./

BOB: Or turn into a piranha.

DILLY: Look, he's a top-notch impresario not a fishmonger or a greengrocer. And I'm here to tell you he just wouldn't. (Tapping the side of her nose.) Trust me. Give it a go.

Blackout.

SCENE TWO

The dress circle bar. N.B. Again, if the budget does not permit, it would be possible to play this scene on an undressed forestage with only some very small adjustments to the dialogue.

JIMMY *and* **BOB** *sit at a table.* **DAN** *strides around opposite them. If First & Last were Laurel & Hardy they would be quivering in their shoes.*

DAN: *(Going nuts and bananas.)* I just couldn't believe my eyes when I saw the stage manager's report. Eight minutes! What *do* you think you're up to? How dare you! How dare you make my show overrun! My audiences pay good money not to have to tax themselves. If everyone decided to put eight minutes on the show it'd run till bloody midnight. B'time the show came down the pubs'd be closed. You could start a riot.

BOB: But it was a good eight minutes.

DAN: I don't care a monkey's fart! You had no permission! No permission!

JIMMY: But the punters even came back early after the intermission/

DAN: I don't want them coming back early. I want them spending money here in the bar.

JIMMY: Yes, but it's the best we've been so far/ And I think people have been really enjoying the experiment/

BOB: Judging by the merriment.

DAN: Experiment! In a summer season! What do you imagine you're playing at?

JIMMY: We're getting Joe Public really involved/

BOB: And your problem with the next show's suddenly solved.

DAN: Solved my backside! You will never dare to rhyme on one of my stages ever again.

BOB: Guv'nor, please, we're mining a new vein/

JIMMY: Found a different way to entertain/

BOB: Have cracked the –

DAN: And you can stop that here and now.

BOB: You said you wanted us to communicate/

JIMMY: Yes, Mr. Sandford, please elucidate.

DAN: I know what I said. But at this precise moment I just can't think straight with you two chiming away.

    Pause.

Driving me up the wall it is! How the punters are finding it funny I just don't know. Now, where was I?

JIMMY: Eight minutes.

DAN: Ah, yes!

BOB: Some matinees we have only added six or seven.

DAN: Only added six or seven? Six or seven! Am I hearing you straight? That could be your whole act if you were a unicyclist.

JIMMY: But you've as good as admitted, Mr. Sandford, so you must have heard, that we've had them wetting themselves with laughter.

DAN: The only place where people wet themselves in Southport, Mr. Last, is when they're in the sea. It's the biggest public lavatory in in this part of Lancashire. Anyhow, just supposing you're right, what about the poor buggers who have to go on after you and follow an act like that? Have you given them a thought? No. Too bloody selfish.

BOB: But our teamwork's improved.

DAN: Your teamwork has, but what about the show as a whole? I'll have you know that some members of the cast have been making representations. And worse, much, much worse. The musicians are agitating to be paid overtime! I can't go throwing money at violinists and drummers. What are you trying to do to me? Pull the plug on my empire?

JIMMY: Of course not, we're…all we're doing is expanding on what was, after all, your bright idea. You should be pleased as Punch.

DAN: Look, Mr. Last, the whole point of requiring you to speak in rhyme was to sharpen up your act – not to become it.

BOB: But our patter's improved, Guv'nor, and our cross-talk.

DAN: It has. It has. But I don't want a wordy act. This is summer. This is Southport God-damn-it.

JIMMY: But it's witty.

DAN: Witty? Who's ever heard of wit beside the seaside?! In any case, I have singers who sing in rhyme. Why pay two salaries to two comics to do it without the bloody music?!

> *Short pause as* **DAN** *tries to calm himself, after which he continues in a more restrained but more ominous tone.*

I've absolutely and utterly had enough, gentlemen.

BOB: It wasn't our idea, you know.

DAN: What d'you mean?

BOB: It was Dilly who thought it might go down a storm.

DAN: Oh was it?

BOB: Yes, she said she thought you'd approve.

DAN: Oh did she?

BOB: Aye.

    Pause.

DAN: Well, let me tell you something, Mr. First. Dilys is a soubrette. Do you know what a soubrette is? (Answering his own question.) A soubrette is someone who sings and dances but can't really do either. Why would you listen to her?

    He glares at **BOB**, *daring him to speak the unspoken.*

BOB: No…no reason especially. We just thought…but you're right. We made the decision. We have to live with the consequences.

DAN: Damn right you do.

JIMMY: And what are they, Mr. Sandford?

    Hold.

DAN: Well…given all the circumstances…um, I suspect we should try to find a compromise.

BOB: That's very generous, Guv'nor.

DAN: Good. Then you do as I say and we'll have one.

BOB: Oh.

DAN: But my bones, my theatrical bones, are telling me we need a new approach. Mr. Last…when you're thinking up a routine, or a sketch, or just a gag, what frame of mind do you put yourself into? I mean, what's your rule of thumb?

JIMMY: I've never really thought about it. But I suppose my view is that entertainment is like sugar. You can have brown sugar and you can have white sugar. (An afterthought.) Or you can have saccharin I suppose. I prefer brown.

DAN: Do you now?

JIMMY: Ideally, I like humour that's got…something behind it.

DAN: What, satire? Not bloody satire! Right, right, now we're getting to the root of what's been the trouble. What about you, Mr. First? What triggers your ideas?

BOB: What I like to do…(he fishes in his pocket.)…

DAN: (To himself.) …satire…

BOB: ...is put a knotted handkerchief over me head – like so – and imagine I'm sitting on a beach, in the sun, in a deckchair. Then I think, what sort of act would tempt me to drag myself out of this deckchair, put it back in the stack, take the flask and bags back to the B & B, and then pay money I haven't really got to come and see me. So I imagine myself out front in my socks and sandals, watching myself on stage making me forget I'd ever struggled to put up a deckchair. And on wet days, when there's no beach to get up from, I provide the sunshine. And that's my act. Well, it used to be until Jimmy came along.

DAN: So...a clear winner. That's the way forward...

(BOB grins, JIMMY looks daggers at him.)

...if you want me to consider you for pantomime that is. Do we understand each other?

BOB: (After a beat.) I think we do.

DAN: Is that unanimous?

JIMMY: Yeah.

DAN: Right, for the next show then, you go the deckchair route. Which means coming up with something that's more knockabout and less wordy.

JIMMY: (Dry.) Like what?

DAN: Look, you signed the contract. You're the funny men. Make me laugh along the dotted line. And offstage... (Pausing for effect.) I need you to step up your rhyming.

BOB: Oh, but Guv'nor...

DAN: No 'buts'. From now on, you rhyme wherever you are, whoever you're with, even if you're not together. You'll be brilliant b'time I've finished with you.

BOB: But what if one of us happens to be, say, in a bank? Or in a church even? Not that we're likely to be in either.

DAN: Wherever you are I said. You'll be like walking posters for the show. Go on now, off you go and get rhyming.

(They make to go.)

No. We'll start from now, shall we?

(Pause. The men look as if they're about to rebel, then.)

BOB: Goodbye Guv'nor, we'll see you at rehearsals/

JIMMY: Barring any unforeseen reversals.

(BOB grabs JIMMY's arm and pulls him off before he can elaborate.

DAN lets out a huge sigh, looks about him, picks up his briefcase and makes to go.

There is a noise off.)

DAN: Who's there?

DILLY: *(Off.)* It's only little me.

(DILLY enters tentatively, sorting some songbooks. She is dressed casually, but to kill. They speak in hushed tones.)

I dropped my music.

DAN: Oh, did you?

DILLY: What's been going on, Dan?

DAN: As if you didn't know.

DILLY: What's that supposed to mean?

DAN: The boys tell me they were rhyming in the show at your suggestion.

DILLY: You're not angry with me, are you?

DAN: No. I'm bloody furious.

DILLY: Oh, Danny, don't be like that.

DAN: Don't try to get round me. You had no business overruling the stage manager. He's got quite enough on his plate with those bloody jugglers losing their rings all the time, without you making him throw another paddy.

DILLY: I thought it would help the show.

DAN: *I* say what helps the show!

DILLY: It wasn't actually my idea, you know.

DAN: Who's was it then?

DILLY: It was that boy's.

DAN: What boy?

DILLY: Teddy. The one I told you about who's itching to be a stage manager.

63

DAN: Huh! He'll be lucky now.

DILLY: Well, he suggested it, and I just said to Bob and Jim that it might... *just* be worth thinking about.

DAN: It wasn't.

DILLY: Please don't be too mad at them, Daniel. I'm sure they thought it was for the best.

DAN: That's all very well, Dilly, but why wasn't I informed? Why did I have to read it in the stage manager's report?

DILLY: I imagine they were looking to see if it worked before –

DAN: I mean, why didn't *you* tell me? I thought you were my early warming system.

DILLY: I'm not a spy, Dan.

DAN: I didn't say spy. I said – I meant – helpmate.

DILLY: So you really, really think it didn't work?

DAN: Not in my book.

DILLY: Except that it did. If I were you, I'd be really pleased with my coaching methods.

DAN: I'll tell you what pleases me.

DILLY: What?

DAN: You, Dilly. All fresh faced and fired up.

DILLY: That's nice.

(Awkward pause.)

So...have you given them the push?

DAN: Course I haven't. This late in the season I'd be hard put to find a decent replacement, but I can't tell them that. Why do you ask?

DILLY: I...I just thought you might be thinking of Eddie & Freddie.

DAN: You'd like me to?

DILLY: No...no I wouldn't.

DAN: Good, because I'd rather not do them a favour if I don't have to.

DILLY: No, I think...I think Bob and Jimmy have got something really original. Thanks to you, of course. They could really go somewhere.

DAN: What, outside my empire you mean?

DILLY: Well, eventually perhaps. But they haven't yet played your Hippodrome.

DAN: And they won't, if they don't buck up their ideas.

DILLY: And nor have I.

DAN: Give it time, darling. Give it time.

> *He holds out his hand. She takes it.*

You coming back to the Queen's Arms for a…a spot of luncheon?

> *She thinks for a moment and then nods her head.*

Well, you go first. Better not be seen walking out together. And I'll bring up the rear…so to speak.

> **DILLY** *waggles her bottom as she disappears.*
>
> **DAN** *looks after her approvingly, and then turns his attention to look at some of the posters of previous shows equally as approvingly [or alternatively walks to the edge of the stage and surveys his theatre with the same measure of approval.] before quickly glancing at his watch and exiting.*

SCENE THREE

The digs. All is quiet apart from the occasional squawk of a seagull. Then the front door is heard to open and close. Voices off, following which **TEDDY** *enters the parlour, ushered in by* **ROSE**.

ROSE *is being as cheerful as she possible can, though it is evident that she is perturbed. It is also evident that* **TEDDY** *is not the animated boy he was previously. Yet although his movement and speech have slowed a little it is clear when he speaks that his mind is as lively as ever.*

ROSE: You come and sit over here in mummy's chair.

> *She leads him to the armchair.*

Now, I've got a little treat for you.

> *She goes to the sideboard.*

Shut your eyes.

> *She takes out a small packet and puts it behind her back.*

What do you think I've got you?

TEDDY: Some stamps.

ROSE: No.

TEDDY: An old newspaper.

ROSE: No. One more guess.

TEDDY: A real live parrot.

ROSE: Now you're being silly. No, Mummy's got you...for being a very brave boy... *(Taking her hand from behind her back.)* ...some... open your eyes....

TEDDY: Wine gums! Oh, fanks, Mum!

ROSE: You deserve them. All that poking about you had to put up with.

TEDDY: *(Opening the packet.)* Am I going to be all right, Mum?

ROSE: 'Course you are. The doctor was very pleased. Now, you see how long you can make one of those last. What were you last time?

TEDDY: A junior gumster.

ROSE: Right, now see if you can make it last ten more minutes and be a senior gumster.

TEDDY: I bet I can.

ROSE: I bet you can't.

TEDDY: How much?

ROSE: Now, we don't do bets, do we?

TEDDY: Mr. Last gambles. So does Mr. First sometimes.

ROSE: I know. Men aren't perfect, Teddy.

TEDDY: Are you going to become Mrs First, Mum?

ROSE: 'Course I'm not! Why would I do that? He's just a very friendly guest.

TEDDY: I like Mr. Last more.

ROSE: Well, that's nice!

TEDDY: It's what I fink.

ROSE: Think. Why do you anyway?

TEDDY: Reminds me of my father.

ROSE: Your father? *(Looking towards the photographs on the wall.)* You've never met your father.

TEDDY: I can see what he looks like in the picture.

ROSE: But that's in black and white. Your father's ginger for heaven's sake. And they don't look anything like each other. Not the slightest. I mean, they're different heights.

TEDDY *retreats into his shell.*

Oh, I'm sorry, little sunshine. This is not the time to talk…family history, is it?

TEDDY: When is, Mum?

ROSE: When you're old enough, that's when. Now, let's give you a lie down for half an hour.

(She helps him to his room as.)

That walk must have really taken it out of you. I hold my hands up here. We should have got a taxi. I know. Mum's really sorry. Come on now, young soldier. Let's get you tucked in.

They go into the front room.

Silence, again only punctuated by a solitary seagull.

Then the front door is heard to open. Voices off, from which emerges.

BOB: *(Off.)* Do you think the coast is clear?/

JIMMY: *(Off.)* Yeah, as clear as a good beer/ Well, as far as I can hear/ But if that ruddy seagull would put a sock in its beak/ I might be able to hear someone speak/

BOB: *(Off.)* I think they must still be out at surgery/

JIMMY: *(Off.)* I'd swear they are, except I don't want to commit perjury/

BOB: Mind the way then, Lasty, I'll go firsty.

BOB *appears from the hall on a bicycle, and rides around the parlour as best he can.*

Oh, this is the life!/ The wind in your hair/ The trees flashing by/ No trouble and strife/ No, never a care/ Fresh air by the cartload/ *(Coming to a sudden and unexpected halt.)* And ruts in the road.

JIMMY *cycles on after him.*

JIMMY: If you're lucky you'll see me at Herne Hill/ I'm one of the racers you know/ I sprint round the track/ When behind I attack/ And when in front I don't know where to go. Whooooo!/

BOB: I'd get those brakes fixed if I were you/

JIMMY: *(Pointedly.)* It's all right, I've got a screwdriver/

BOB: You're just jealous/

JIMMY: No, just a survivor/

BOB: *(After a beat.)* Rose would go crackers if she could see us/

ROSE: *(Off.)* I can hear you.

BOB: Oh Gawd.

> *He dismounts rapidly.* **JIMMY** *follows suit.*
>
> **ROSE** *enters and stands for the moment taking in the sight of the two men with their bicycles.*

ROSE: Do men never grow up? You don't need to answer. It's not a question.

> **BOB** *goes to speak.*

I hope those wheels aren't muddy.

BOB: No, no, we've...we've just picked these up from pawn shop/ They're for our new act. This is a prop.

ROSE: Well, I'm not at all keen for you to go rehearsing here this morning. I'm trying to give Teddy a little bit of a rest.

TEDDY: *(Off, calling.)* I don't mind. They can rehearse in there if they like.

ROSE: Children do undermine you, don't they?

JIMMY: *(Calling.)* Hello there, Teddy.

TEDDY: *(Off.)* Hello, Mr. Last. I've almost finished your wireless.

JIMMY: Oh, good to hear it's nearly ready/

TEDDY: *(Off.)* And I'm gonna let you have it half price 'cos I messed up your act.

JIMMY: No, no, I won't hear of it, and that's a fact/ (Changing his tone.) Anyway, you did nothing of the sort. More important, did it all go okay today?

TEDDY: *(Off.)* I think so, fank you.

> **JIMMY** *mouths 'Did it?' to* **ROSE** *who nods her head from side to side as if to say 'Yes and no.'* **JIMMY** *pulls a face,* **BOB** *looks away.* **TEDDY** *continues, off.*

May I ask what's the new act going to be?

JIMMY: I'm sure you've got other things on your mind, Teddy.

TEDDY: *(Off.)* No I 'aven't.

ROSE: Yes you have.

> **TEDDY** *appears in the doorway.*

TEDDY: No I 'aven't.

68

ROSE: Oh Teddy!

BOB: You won't win, Rosie.

ROSE: Come on then. Come and sit over here.

TEDDY: I'm feeling a bit better now anyway. I think it's the rhyming that's doing it.

ROSE: *(Huffily.)* I'm sorry I can't rhyme for you.

TEDDY: *(As near to tongue in cheek as he can manage.)* You are a rhyme, Mum.

ROSE: Now, don't set me off.

    TEDDY *sits in the armchair.*

TEDDY: Why have you got a lady's bike?

BOB: 'Cos I'm going to be a lady.

    TEDDY *giggles.*

I am.

ROSE: Are you?

BOB: Yeah.

ROSE: What, dress up you mean?

BOB: Of course dress up.

ROSE: Not in my clothes you're not.

BOB: Don't worry yourself, for goodness sake. We have a whole costume department/ Well, we have a wardrobe mistress and a part time assistant, who'll no doubt be able to find me a garment.../ With a suitable escarpment.

ROSE: And where d'you get this desire to dress up?

BOB: Look, I'm still Bob. Still the man you know...you know. That's the gag/

ROSE: What is?

JIMMY: Him in drag.

BOB: That's it. 'Cept in this case I'll be the mother-in-law figure/

JIMMY: Only bigger/

BOB: *(Ignoring this.)* Then we can bring out all the mother-in-law jokes.../

ROSE: ...lovely...

BOB: …though Jimmy and Dilly's characters are not married, they're just doing breaststrokes/ (Quickly.) But the overall joke/ The masterstroke/ Is that I'm gonna be Jimmy's mother not Dilly's/ Who in the sketch we're calling Billy and Lily/ And I'm playing gooseberry to make sure Lily doesn't take advantage of my Billy/ As might happen in say…um..

JIMMY: Piccadilly.

ROSE: And I suppose you're called Milly?

JIMMY: That's a good idea actually.

BOB: But do you get it?

ROSE: I do, I do, and it could be the best thing since sliced bread, to coin a phrase…but I thought you said Mr. Sandford was requiring something a little more visual.

BOB: It *is* visual. What do you think the bikes are for?/

JIMMY: And what about an overdressed, male mother-in-law?

ROSE: Yes, but I don't see how it's going to be knockabout.

JIMMY: Well, we'll all go for a ride/ And try not to collide/ And have a picnic lunch/ Until mother throws a punch/ And Billy, who was feeling chipper/ Gets slapped by a kipper/ And food gets thrown…/ (Almost as an aside.) Not custard pies but, you know, bit of slosh. But not too much. We're not into slosh… And Billy gets his head stuck down the horn of a portable gramophone/ And Milly, let's call her, who isn't worth tuppence/ Gets a justified come-uppance/ And … punch line.

BOB: D'you like it, Teddy?

TEDDY: Yes, I fink…

ROSE: …think…

TEDDY: …it's gonna be super-duper.

ROSE: I'm not convinced about the gramophone though, because it would be very difficult to --

JIMMY: There's no gramophone. I just needed a rhyme!

ROSE: Oh, right. And is this for the first half or the second half?

JIMMY: First, isn't it, First?

BOB: Yes, it's first, Last.

ROSE: And for the second?

BOB: We're not there yet.

ROSE: I thought you started rehearsing next week.

BOB: We're trying not to fret/

JIMMY: Or sweat/

BOB: Or tell our soubrette/

JIMMY: Not to get too upset/

BOB: Or irate/

JIMMY: If the script is late/

ROSE: And what about *her* bike?

BOB: She's borrowing one from her landlady. Apparently, where bikes are concerned, the woman's nervous in the extreme/ And hasn't ridden since she flew over the handlebars and came down on her two scoops of vanilla ice cream.

TEDDY: Miss Williams doesn't need to get herself all upset.

JIMMY: Why's that, Teddy?

TEDDY: 'Cos I've got an idea.

General groans.

BOB: Here we go.

ROSE: I've had enough of this, Teddy, I've really had enough.

BOB: *(Heavily.)* Go on then, lad/ Tell us about this idea you've had.

TEDDY: All right. But you will take it serious?

JIMMY: We'll take it serious. Promise.

TEDDY: Right then, what if, in the second half, you start the sketch the same, 'cept that it's another day and Milly has not changed one little bit? I'll tell you, the best fing about Milly is that she's a collector. The worst fing, is that she collects mousetraps. And so the scene starts with you having sneaked out of the house to meet Lily in a secret meeting place. Or so you fink! Then what happens is that just as Billy and Lilly are about to cycle away together to find a nice quiet picnic spot, Milly roars onto the stage on a motorbike. With a sidecar.

Stunned silence.

A sidecar from which her long lost husband used to sell wet fish. Though it's been cleaned since. And Milly offers Lily a lift on the pillion and you a lift in sidecar, Mr. Last, so she can keep an eye on your both. BUT…the sidecar goes off of its own accord before you can get in it. So you all chase after it and bring it back. Then the motorbike starts up when there's no one on it but stops quickly when Milly shoots it with her husband's old service revolver. And then starts up again with another shot. And so on till the audience is crying with laughter. They'd not be real bullets.

Pause.

ROSE: I think you might have a temperature.

JIMMY: It's a great idea, Teddy, but there's no time to do it/

BOB: And if we tried we'd be likely to screw it.

TEDDY: I could make it work. With a few electrical motors and fings. Old windscreen wiper motors from a scrap yard would probably be enough. Wouldn't cost hardly anyfing.

ROSE: But you're not up to it, darling.

TEDDY: I am, I am. It's just what I need. And I haven't heard from Miss Williams yet about that Saturday job so I've got all the time in the world. Go on, please. You've worked in a garage, Mr. Last, you know it could be done. It only needs a rubbish-y motorbike. And if you can't find a sidecar at a scrap yard, I could make you one, 'cos that's what stage managers do…don't they?

BOB *and* **JIMMY** *look at each other as if they might be prepared to suspend their disbelief.*

It ain't wordy.

Lights out.

SCENE FOUR

(In the darkness a motorbike is heard to roar onto the stage with a hoot and a bang or two and a general cacophony of noise. Audience laughter. Motorbike engine is turned off. Muffled dialogue. Sounds of panic. More laughter. Motorbike engine starts again. A gun fires. Motorbike engine stops. Laughter. Motorbike engine starts up again. A gun fires again. Motorbike engine continues. Another shot. Motorbike is heard to crash. Gales of laughter.

Lights go up on First & Last's dressing room. **JIMMY** *and* **BOB** *enter in their costumes, almost tearing them off. BOB is dressed rather like a pantomime dame, though without the heavy make-up, and* **JIMMY** *as a gormless young man.)*

BOB: How we got through that show/ I do not know!/

JIMMY: If the stage manager hadn't had hysterics, it might have helped the situation/

BOB: They need to put that twat on medication/ But there's no disputing/ That bloody motorbike needs shooting/ And not just with blanks/

JIMMY: It was like a tank/ It's cut my knee/

BOB: Well, what about me?/ If you want the particulars/ I got a whack in the testiculars.

JIMMY: I take it you don't think we'll get away with it?

BOB: Don't be so ridiculous, that's absolutely out of the question/

JIMMY: Well, you agreed to Teddy's suggestion/

BOB: Oh, my fault now, is it? You did nothing I suppose – except go to town with your little screwdriver/ And give the scrap-yard man a fiver/ Which we hadn't got/ And for what?/ To get the sack/

JIMMY: It may not come to that/

BOB: Oh come off it! This time we've blown it good and proper/ First & Last has…

JIMMY and **BOB:** *(Together.)* Come a cropper.

JIMMY: Bugger, bugger, bugger.

BOB: You can rhyme that yourself.

JIMMY: Don't know why we're bothering any more. If we're out in the cold, what the hell's it matter?

BOB: It worked though. You must admit it made us a top-notch double.

JIMMY: Enough for us give it another go, somewhere else in the country?

BOB: I don't think so. Do you?

JIMMY: No…

BOB: Life has got to be better than this.

JIMMY: Don't put money on it.

BOB: Will you go back to your black-faced act?

JIMMY: No, no, I've outgrown that. I'll try something a little more unusual.

BOB: Oh, something funny then?

JIMMY: At least I won't have to listen to you eat.

A beat.

BOB: Well, I probably won't be needing these falsies again. More's the pity. I think I'd really stand out as a dame.

JIMMY: Look, are you sure Sandford was in? I didn't see him in his usual place.

BOB: I'm only going by what Michael Magic said. Said he thought he saw him in the wings on prompt side at one point. But I had other things on my mind. Like a frigging motorbike! I mean, try explaining this to your mates in the pub. I got fired because a motorbike and sidecar had more presence of mind than I did!

There is a knock on the dressing room.

JIMMY: Come in.

DAN enters looking stern.

BOB: Ev'ning, Guv'nor.

DAN: What kind of stupid, risky act was that, boys?

JIMMY: You okayed it, Mr. Sandford.

DAN: I okayed the motorcycle, against my better judgement I'm here to say, but I didn't okay any stupid tricks with it.

JIMMY: We thought we'd give you a surprise/

DAN: Surprise? You damn nearly ran me over out there in the wings.

BOB: Don't we get marks for enterprise?/

DAN: That motorbike could have landed in the orchestra pit. We could have had a few smashed instruments to pay for, not to mention a dead musician or two.

JIMMY: But as it was, it only hit the greenery/ Which was just a bit of old scenery.

DAN: That's my set you're talking about, lad!

JIMMY: But we used it in the last show/

DAN: That's what scenery's for.

BOB: It wasn't our idea, you know/

DAN: I suppose it's that boy's fault again, is it? What's his name?

BOB: Teddy.

JIMMY: He's not to blame/ We just thought it was a great concept.

DAN: And that's the one place where I agree with you.

JIMMY: What?

BOB: Eh…?

DAN: It's brilliant. A brilliant idea. I know it didn't work tonight, but with a little tweaking we've got a massive act on our hands here, boys.

BOB: Fuck a duck, are you serious?

DAN: That I am. And I could see an act like that fitting very nicely into panto this winter. Possibly at the Hippodrome. If you boys were interested.

BOB: Interested? Blimey! We're   **JIMMY:** You bet your backside!
delirious!

BOB: (Genuine.) It's better than working down a mine, Guv'nor.

DAN: If they'd have you. 'Cos it's not nice out there in the wide world at the moment, is it, boys? So remember that when you're negotiating your contract. I'm not made of money, you know.

BOB: And…and would we be working with Dilly?

DAN: 'Ccourse you would. She's…well, truth is, in entertainment terms, you can't really make a silk purse out of a sow's ear, but if you cook it long enough it's perfectly edible.

   Embarrassed pause.

BOB: So what did you think of the rest of the show?

JIMMY: Yes, what about our sketch/ In the first half?/ Did it make you laugh?/ Or retch?

DAN: No, not retch, it was very good, very good. And I loved the punch line. (He chuckles at the thought.) Didn't see that coming at all. And I thought the piece showed off Miss Williams' good qualities very well. Very well. In fact, the only place tonight where I thought you boys were still not smacking the donkey on the nose was with the pathos. Your onion's now gone from one extremity to the other. Yes, we need sentimentality to help put laughter into perspective, but we don't need to milk the tears so much that the laughs disappear over the bloody horizon, now do we?

There is a knock on the door. **JIMMY** *and* **BOB** *continue to get changed as the scene continues.*

BOB: *(Calling.)* Yes?

DILLY: *(Off.)* It's only little me.

BOB: Oh, come in, Dill.

The door opens slightly and **DILLY** *puts her head around the door nervously.*

DILLY: And little them.

She opens the door and lets **ROSE** *through.* **ROSE** *is pushing* **TEDDY** *in a wheelchair.*

BOB: Make way, make way! Do we all know each other?

DILLY: Hello, Mr. Sandford.

DAN: Hello, Dilys. You were on top form, my girl.

DILLY: That's very kind of you, Mr. Sandford.

BOB: And this is Rosemary Hoskins, our landlady.

DAN: Oh, Mrs Hoskins, I'm very pleased to meet you. I've heard so much about you.

ROSE: That's nice.

DAN: And this, I take it, is Teddy.

TEDDY shrinks in his chair, expecting the worst.

Now, let me get this straight. You're the boy who suggested that these two mugs should rhyme on stage?

TEDDY nods.

And you're the boy who can make a motorcycle go of its own accord?

TEDDY nods again.

DILLY: But he *is* only a boy, Mr. Sandford. You can't expect too much…

DAN: *(Ignoring her completely.)* Let me shake hands with a genius. What a cracking idea, lad. Got any more up there, have you?

TEDDY: Yes, well, that's what makes me fink I could be a stage manager.

DAN: With ideas like that, you could be a fellow impresario. You'd obviously have to get yourself a little bit better first, and get some money behind you, but in the meantime I'm of the opinion we might be able to find you a little something to do here at the Winter Gardens. Don't you, Dill?

DILLY: I do, yes, yes.

DAN: Making and mending props perhaps? What do you think, boys?

BOB: Great.   **JIMMY:** Just what he needs.

DAN: And you, Mrs Hoskins?

ROSE: Yes…that would be perfect.

DAN: What d'you say, Teddy?

TEDDY: You won't regret it, Mr. Sandford.

DAN: I'm sure I won't. *(Slight pause.)* Now, we can't have you using up all your supplies of lemonade, Bob. So I say we adjourn to the bar to celebrate the coaching methods of yours truly.

A babble of banter.

Dilys, go tell Otto he's got to keep open.

DILLY: *(Sing song but with her nose slightly out of joint.)* Will do.

She goes.

DAN: Drinks on me everybody!

General agreement.

ROSE: How will we get Teddy up to the bar?

BOB: We'll carry the chair/ Upstairs/

JIMMY: I'll push him to the foyer if you like/

BOB: No, no, on your bike/ I'm pushing, eh Rosie?

ROSE: Yes, your job.

BOB: We've turned the corner, flower. Big kiss for big Bob?

ROSE: Look, you keep those thoughts to yourself, or you'll lose your privileges.

Laughter.

DAN: Come on, let's go.

JIMMY: And get blotto/

BOB: Up in the grotto/

JIMMY: With Otto/

BOB: Then play some lotto/

JIMMY: Eat some risotto/

BOB: And live by the motto…/

DAN: And you can stop that right away!

JIMMY: But we've got the hang.

BOB: We're a gang.

JIMMY: We're a team

BOB: We're a scream

DAN: You bloody are. And I'll be screaming in minute. Don't you realize, my friends? You're there. Electricity at last! We did it! Congratulations. It's over. No more rhyming!

Handshakes and whoops all round. In her excitement, **ROSE** *gives* **DAN** *a smothering hug. It is then that they realize they've left* **TEDDY** *out of the loop.*

Oh, you not celebrating, young Teddy?

TEDDY: *(Lacklustre.)* No.

DAN: But you're on your way to becoming a stage manager, lad.

TEDDY: I know. But I liked the rhyming.

Fade out.

SCENE FIVE

The digs. **JIMMY** *and* **BOB** *sit in silence finishing the remains of their breakfast. Between mouthfuls they look across to* **TEDDY**, *who lies asleep on the sofa with a blanket over him.* **ROSE** *appears in the kitchen doorway wiping her hands on a tea towel. She looks at* **TEDDY** *anxiously then disappears without a glance at the men.)*

BOB: What you planning on this morning?

JIMMY: Nothing. You?

BOB: Same.

They return to their own worlds. **ROSE** *then re-enters and crosses to the table. They converse in lowered voices, to avoid waking* **TEDDY**.

ROSE: Everything all right, boys?

BOB: Just delicious, Rosie.

ROSE: *(To* **JIMMY**.*)* I'm sorry there wasn't enough skin off the milk for two.

     BOB *grins.*

JIMMY: I wouldn't have enjoyed it. Not with Teddy lying there.

ROSE: It would have only gone to waste. His tummy just can't take anything at the moment.

JIMMY: I know this is none of my business, Rose, but shouldn't he be in hospital?

ROSE: What, Southport Hospital? Do you want to finish him off?

JIMMY: What about calling the doctor?

ROSE: *(Lowering her voice still further.)* The doctor knows. He says there's nothing they can do. And now he's caught this nasty bug on top of everything else...

JIMMY: But, surely, there might just be something –

ROSE: I know what I'm doing. He belongs here, not in a colourless hospital.

BOB: Wouldn't he be better in his own bed though?

JIMMY: Mmm.

ROSE: I know he's taking up your space, boys. But I need to keep an eye on him. If you don't like it I'll knock something off the rent.

BOB: No, no, no, no, no.   **JIMMY:** Wouldn't hear of it.

ROSE: I'll take your plates then.

BOB: Thanks, Rose.

ROSE: It's a lovely, sunny day. Doesn't look like you'll need to do the extra show.

BOB: That's just as well. The fire officer's being very stingy with the amount of petrol he's letting me have for the motorbike. If we get too many laughs it'll conk out mid sketch.

ROSE: *(Going into the kitchen.)* Oh well, season's nearly over. Pantomime next, is it?

JIMMY: Yep. All signed and sealed. Well, nearly.

ROSE: *(Off.)* You know, I always thought you had something.

BOB: We're going places, flower.

ROSE: *(Off.)* So you say, Bob.

BOB: We'll not be that far away. I'll be able to pop over and see you on a Sunday.

ROSE: *(Off.)* For your steak and dumplings you mean?

BOB: To…to see whether we're still up on that wall.

ROSE: *(Off.)* You'll be on a wall somewhere, never you fear.

> *At this moment* **TEDDY** *turns over and gives a little groan.*

BOB: I think you need to come and have a quick look at him, Rosemary.

> **ROSE** *strides back in, goes to* **TEDDY** *and peers at him closely.*

ROSE: No, he's…he's fine. He's breathing.

> *She looks around aimlessly.*

I just don't know what to do with myself.

BOB: Come and sit down and have a cup of tea with us.

ROSE: No, no, I've got to keep going. Keep active.

> *She goes this way and that, doing nothing in particular.*

JIMMY: Look…I'll leave you both to it.

> *He gets up.*

I'll go and view the photos in your lavatory.

ROSE: There's no need to be crude, Mr. Last.

JIMMY: Sorry. Call me if you need any help.

ROSE: Thank you.

> **JIMMY** *goes. Awkward moment.*

BOB: If you won't sit down, I'll stand up.

> **ROSE** *instinctively turns away from him.*

So…what did the doctor actually tell you, flower?

ROSE: Please don't 'flower' me. I'm not in a flowery mood.

BOB: You don't need to tell me if you don't care to.

ROSE: It's just a matter of time. His stomach can't process anything. So…

BOB: Right.

ROSE: It's not right.

BOB: No.

ROSE: *(A whisper.)* But better that God takes him now, before he loses his innocence.

BOB: If you say so.

    Pause.

And what will you do with yourself? You know.

ROSE: I'm beyond caring. I'll think about that down the track. What about you? Will you really come to visit?

BOB: I will. I will. Every Sunday without fail.

ROSE: If I'm here.

BOB: What do you mean by that?

ROSE: I might just sell up and…go on a cruise…until the money runs out.

    BOB *nods away but can't think what to say. He is saved by* **TEDDY** *groaning again. They both go to him.*

BOB: Rosemary, Jimmy's right, it does seem to me he needs some proper medical –

ROSE: I make the decisions here.

BOB: I understand.

ROSE: No you don't. You see, I'm the one who's been waiting all this time for a miracle to happen. But it hasn't. No, that's not true. The miracle is that I've had him for so long. But we all need another miracle, don't we? One's never enough.

BOB: Do you really think he can't hear us?

ROSE: Doctor says he can't.

BOB: Hey there, Teddy. Act's going great guns you know. Getting all the laughs, and more. And that motorbike is…boy, what an entrance you've given me! And apart from the first time, all those tricks have worked like a dream. You know, I was thinking, we could perhaps do something like that with a Model T Ford. And have the back fall off or something. Eh?

    There is no reaction from **TEDDY.**

ROSE: See.

BOB: But he still might be able to hear.

ROSE: Look, I've tried. I've tried, Bob.

    BOB *walks away.*

I have, I've sat here and read to him from his book of cartoons and not one of them has raised a smile. And we've crisscrossed the whole of the damn British Empire via his stamps. And I've talked him though at least half of his collection of lovebirds and parrots but he hasn't even –

There is a knock on the door.

Oh no! Who can that be? What a time to come knocking!

She goes out. **BOB** *wanders around aimlessly, then looks off in the direction* **JIMMY** *has exited, almost wishing him back.*

Voices off. The street door is heard to close.

ROSE: *(Off.)* You've got a visitor, Bob.

BOB: Oh, aye. Who could that be?

DILLY: *(Off.)* Only little me.

BOB: My goodness! Hey, come in.

DILLY *enters, looking fashionably casual.*

What brings you here?

DILLY: You're not on the phone, that's what brings me here!

ROSE *reappears.*

ROSE: If you could keep your voice down a little.

DILLY: *(Seeing* **TEDDY***.)* Oh, the little mite! Bless him! Has he not been responding to the treatment then?

ROSE: No…not responding.

DILLY: Oh, you must be pulling your hair out.

ROSE: I'm wearing a wig. So, what can this big lump here do for you?

DILLY: I've come with a message, which I would have conveyed some other way, if there'd been another way.

BOB: Why couldn't it wait till the half?

DILLY: 'Cos there's not going to be a half. For you and Jimmy.

BOB: What?!

DILLY: Don't worry. This is good news.

JIMMY *enters, drying his hands on his handkerchief.*

JIMMY: Oh, hello, Dilly, what you doing here?

DILLY: I'm just telling Bob. Mr. Sandford wants you to skip the shows today.

JIMMY: He does what?!

DILLY: If you listen I'll explain. We've got to be quick anyway.

JIMMY: Go on then.

DILLY: I don't know if you know that the BBC's doing an outside broadcast from the Hippodrome tonight.

JIMMY: Yeah, we'd sort of got wind of it.

DILLY: Well, Mr. Funny Man top of the bill fell down some stairs last night, pissed out of his bloody mind – pardon the puns – and he's in hospital with concussion and a broken leg.

BOB: Oh that's fantastic!

JIMMY: You mean the Guv'nor's asking us to replace him?

DILLY: Lucky you, eh?

BOB: But what about the motorbike?

> **TEDDY** *stirs. Nobody notices.*

DILLY: You don't need a motorbike. He thinks you're first-class now, with or without a motorbike…

BOB: Good Gawd.

DILLY: …and it's too visual for the wireless anyways.

JIMMY: Words! Heaven be praised, he wants words!

DILLY: More than that, he wants you there, like right now, with one eight minute act to finish off the show – as the BBC's only broadcasting the second half.

ROSE: But what about 'Follies on Parade', what happens to that?

DILLY: He's got a replacement, just for today.

ROSE: Who?

DILLY: Eddie & Freddie.

BOB: Bloody boots!

JIMMY: But why move everyone around? They've done radio, they could slot straight in over in Liverpool. Save a bother here.

DILLY: Well, I'm only guessing of course…

JIMMY: Of course.

DILLY: …but I think he doesn't feel they deserve a lift up. They've had their chance. If you stick by Mr. Sandford he'll stick by you. But you've got to be there no later than the afternoon run through. And

I've a taxi waiting outside to take you to the station. You should just make it if you catch the next train. That's if you're up for it.

BOB: Oh, Dill, Dill, you are the bringer of glad tidings! Isn't she Jimmy?

JIMMY: Fantastic, Dill.

BOB: Come here, give us a hug.

DILLY: You can leave that for another time, Bob First. We're in a rush.

ROSE: You hear that?

JIMMY: What do we need? What do we need?

DILLY: Nothing really. Just a funny hat perhaps? And a costume, but even that doesn't matter. They've a grand costume department.

BOB: You said it was radio.

DILLY: It is radio. But there's still an audience in the theatre that need to see something. Otherwise they might as well listen to it at home.

JIMMY: Come on, Bob. Let's go get our stuff.

BOB: Yes, partner!

*They go to the bottom of the stairs, where they are stopped by **DILLY**'s voice.*

DILLY: Oh yes. And your band parts if you're going to sing. You'll need those.

*The men do a little soft shoe shuffle together ending with a flourish from **JIMMY** and then rush off up the stairs, with **JIMMY** humming an arpeggio or two as he goes. Pause. Left alone, the women are all too conscious of **TEDDY**'s silent presence.*

ROSE: Like a cup of tea?

DILLY: No thanks, we've got to race. Taxi's throbbing away.

ROSE: Are you going along with them?

DILLY: No, no… Mr. Sandford needs me to hold the show together at this end.

ROSE: Shame there's not another broken leg going.

DILLY: Yes, quite! But…only another couple of months and we'll be rehearsing the Christmas show at the Hippodrome.

ROSE: Got a good part?

DILLY: I'm Principal Girl. Princess Badroulbadour.

ROSE: You deserve it, Dilly.

DILLY: Thank you. And Bob's Widow Twankey…

ROSE: …surprise me…

DILLY: Yes, so he's the Dame and Jimmy's her hopeless son…

ROSE: …Wishee Washee.

DILLY: You've seen it, have you?

ROSE: Yes…I have. Once or twice.

DILLY: Will you come?

ROSE: *(With a nod towards* **TEDDY***.)* Depends.

DILLY: Of course. May I try speaking to him?

ROSE: Please do.

DILLY: Teddy, it's Miss Williams.

> *(***TEDDY*** moves slightly.)*

ROSE: Oooh.

DILLY: Hello, Teddy. Sorry you're feeling poorly. Now what can I tell you? I know, I'm hitting that high C spot on now every night. And we're all doing brilliant in the motorbike scene. And that little stage management job is still open, for whenever you're up to it.

ROSE: He can't hear you, you know.

TEDDY: Yes, I can.

> **ROSE** *freezes and unfreezes in an instant.* **DILLY** *takes two steps back.*

ROSE: Teddy? Teddy, it's Mummy.

TEDDY: I know. *(Moving his head off the pillow as best he can.)* When I called you mummy once you told me not to be so wet.

ROSE: I know, I know. Mum then. It's Mum.

> *She hugs him desperately.*

ROSE: How are you feeling, my little sunshine?

TEDDY: Not very well. Can't breathe very well.

ROSE: Well then, don't speak. You rest.

TEDDY: Is Mr. Last still here?

ROSE: He's upstairs.

TEDDY: And Mr. First?

ROSE: Same. They're throwing some things in their bags.

TEDDY: Fings? What fings?

DILLY: Props and music and a few clothes. They're doing a radio broadcast tonight.

TEDDY: Ooooh, super! Can we listen?

ROSE: I suppose.

TEDDY: Are they going to rhyme?

DILLY: No, no, not tonight, Teddy.

TEDDY: Oh please, please ask them to, then I'll know it's for me.

DILLY: They just can't…really. It'd be too difficult. In the circumstances.

TEDDY: Will they rhyme for me now then?

ROSE: I would have thought so.

> **DILLY** *is vigorously shaking her head and pointing at her watch.*

Well, maybe. But maybe not. Another time I'm sure.

TEDDY: I see.

> *His head drops and appears to have fallen back to sleep.*

ROSE: Teddy? Teddy? He's not breathing very well.

DILLY: Oh dear oh dear.

ROSE: Did you notice that?

DILLY: What?

ROSE: His breathing stopped for a second and then started again.

DILLY: No, I didn't --

ROSE: Seems alright now though.

DILLY: I'm sure it is.

> **BOB** *and* **JIMMY** *bounce down the stairs with their bags.*

BOB: We're ready!

JIMMY: Take it away, Dill!

BOB: Everything alright?

ROSE: He woke up and asked if you'd rhyme for him.

> **DILLY** *screws up her face and turns her head away anxiously.*

BOB: Really?

JIMMY: I think we could do that for the lad, don't you, Bob?

DILLY: No! No, there's no time.

JIMMY: We'll make time.

DILLY: Look, I'm so sorry, but you just can't. The train won't wait.

JIMMY: Can't we catch the next one?

DILLY: They're actually starting rehearsals in half an hour. You're going to be late as it is.

JIMMY: It's not a Royal Command Performance.

DILLY: It is in Mr. Sandford's mind.

JIMMY: This is just ridiculous!

DILLY: It really is now or never, Jim.

JIMMY: Oh, all right, I suppose we've got to…

BOB: …we have, Jimmy, this is our shot at the big-time…

JIMMY: …I know, I know…

BOB: …may not come again.

JIMMY: I know! It's just that --

ROSE: God, I think he might be going. He keeps holding his breath.

BOB: You must 'phone the doctor, Rose.

ROSE: Alright then. I'll shoot over to Mrs Harris in the blue house.

BOB: It's the right thing to do I'm sure.

ROSE: See you in a minute then. Don't go away.

    She hurries out.

DILLY: I'm so, so sorry, boyos, but we must go, we really, really must go.

JIMMY: Oh no, no! Come on, Bob, let's give him a grandstand finish.

DILLY: Mr. Sandford'll go absolutely ape-shit if you don't turn up. And you know what that'll mean. For all of us.

BOB: That's a point, Jimmy.

JIMMY: But…but think of the lad…it's…it's his last request.

BOB: I am, I know, but you've got to look after yourself in this world.

DILLY: He's right.

BOB: Come on, Jim. Rose'll be back in a second. She's the one that should be with him.

JIMMY: I just can't make you out.

BOB: I'm going, Jim. I'll do the slot on my own if I have to. I'll feed myself the lines. Easy enough.

(JIMMY just glares at him.)

You coming?

JIMMY: No, I'm staying. I'll feed myself the rhymes if I have to. Easy enough.

BOB: He won't hear you.

JIMMY: How do you know? *What* do you know?

BOB: Now, now, flower!

JIMMY: Bugger off, you fat oaf.

BOB: I'm gone, matey.

JIMMY: Good.

BOB: Right then, you stay and join the dole queue. Because you'll be finished here. And blacklisted into the bargain. Coming, Dill?

DILLY: Yes…yes…I'll come to the station with you. Then…then…I'll come back, Jim….to see how…

JIMMY: Don't bother.

DILLY: Right…right, come on, Bob.

> **BOB** *picks up his bag.*

BOB: Last chance, Jimmy.

JIMMY: That's right.

> *He looks toward* **TEDDY***.*

BOB: Bye, Teddy. Good luck, son.

> *He goes to the door.*

Tell Rose… No, don't worry, I'll…no, never mind…

> *He goes.* **DILLY** *follows, though it takes all of her will power to do so.*

JIMMY: I'm here, Teddy.

> *He settles on the end of the sofa.*

End of an era, eh? Can you hear me?

> **TEDDY** *does not stir.*

> *Off in the street, a car door slams and a taxi is heard to drive away.*

Off you go, dear boy. *(To himself.)* The stage manager's beckoning. You've had your eight minutes…or so/ *(To* **TEDDY***.)* Hey, come on, let go/ We're going to be on the radio!/ You and I/ We going to fly/ Through the ether/ In the teeth-a/ The wind/ Because we're destined/ To arrive in a million places/ At the same time/ And light up as many faces/ Who we won't see but who'll think we're sublime/ Cos we will be!

> TEDDY *kicks his feet a fraction but stops almost as quickly as he began.* JIMMY *is pulled up in his tracks. He waits to see if there is any more movement. There isn't.*

But Hollywood can wait. Just for now/ We've made a vow/ Have we not, young wizard?/ That we'll fly on the back of the winged lizard/ Or should I say the dragon?/ All the way to BBC Broadcasting House that's been newly built in London town/ And touch-down on the roof/ Straight on the band wagon!/ Where we'll plant the dragon's sharpest tooth/ Which'll grow into a warrior of great renown/ Who'll protect us from the sharks and the agents and especially the men in suits/ Who can dilute/ A script with one simple utensil/ A pencil!/ But we won't worry about their agendas/ As we're the real cat's whiskers and have splendours/ To rival their little piece of lead/ Don't we now? Because we are the seedbed/ Of ideas. Are we not?/ Because only we know the plot/ So we must keep moving/ Cos moving's soothing/ And tether the dragon/ Beside this flagon/ Of ale/ Which won't fail/ To keep it happy/ Otherwise it might get snappy!/ Now let's make our way down the hatch to the studio below/ Where the magic happens. But…oh!/ It's not a studio, no/ We're in the wrong place/ But what a great mistake to make!/ Forget the censors/ This is a room full of condensers/ And valves and knobs and switches/ Which is/ To say it's not Aladdin's but Teddy's cave/ This is the place where the radio waves/ Come in from studios in other regions/ Manned by Brummies and Bristolians and Glaswegians/ And are in turn beamed out to the whole nation/ To help bring it together – for once – with no need for translation/ Despite the occasional oscillation…

> *At this moment* ROSE *appears in the doorway. She quickly takes in the situation and, after a fleeting look around the room for signs of* BOB *and* DILLY, *walks slowly up behind* JIMMY *as he continues.*

And listen…can you hear?/ It's a miracle all the way from Lancashire/ Here we are, all these miles from home/ And there's a broadcast coming in from the Liverpool Hippodrome/ Can you believe it?!/ BBC Manchester's received it/ And passed the parcel/ For us to pass to Plymouth, Nottingham and Newcastle/ There's plenty of clapping/ So the audience isn't napping/ And, hold on, wait a tick --

> ROSE *puts a hand gently on* JIMMY's *shoulder. He halts for a brief moment and looks up surprised, but resumes his story when cued by* ROSE *mouthing the words 'Don't stop'.*

I know this music/ That's Bob's old signature tune/ And the compère's introducing the last act/ My goodness, it's Bob, it's Mr. First, coming on like a typhoon!/ This'll make an impact/ Across the nation/ As long as everyone's tuned in to the right station/ So what's he going with first?/ I see, well he could do worse.../ Can you hear? I'll say it along with him just to give the signal a boost ...then I got into another queue, thinking it was for bananas. When I arrived at the head of the queue I found I was a blood donor! They pushed a needle into my left arm, my left leg, my right leg. In the end they said, "Come on, quit stalling, where do you keep it?" Boy, they like him/ And he likes them. He's in the swim/ He's in the groove/ Holy Moses, he has improved/

> ROSE *sits beside* TEDDY *and holds his hand, occasionally whispering in his ear as.*

And here's another/ Along with your mother... I've got a nephew – called Teddy – who's just started working as a commercial traveller. He did very well on his first day, got two orders – 'Come in' and 'Get out'. Of course, he has to take the rough with the smooth. At one place they actually threw him out of the side door. Oh! He was furious. He picked himself up and said 'You can't do that to me. I work for a very important firm.' So they took him back in and threw him out of the main entrance.

> *He clicks his fingers.*

You got it! That's my Bob. And now...this is a joke we used to do together/ Which needs a feather/ Light touch because it's about a parrot/ But not the one that swallowed the carrot. I say: 'How is your parrot?' And he says, 'Very well, he not only talks but he's got a great sense of humour.' And I say, 'Why?' Great line that. And he says, 'Well, the minute I walk in the front door, he shouts "Blimey, my husband – blimey, my husband".' I don't expect you'll get that one. But they do. What a belter of a laugh!/

> *He clicks his fingers.*

And that's another.

He clicks his fingers.

And that's another.

He clicks his fingers.

And that's another.

ROSE *gently kisses* **TEDDY** *on the forehead.*

They'll be clambering for his autograph.

Pause.

He's made it, Teddy, he's made it.

Lights fade. Lively play-off music.

THE END.

Printed in the USA
CPSIA information can be obtained
at www.ICGtesting.com
JSHW031714140824
68134JS00038B/3696

9 781913 630461